Helga Fritzsche

Bantams

Husbandry and Care, Diseases, and Breeding
With a Special Chapter on Understanding Bantams

Photos by outstanding animal photographers and drawings
by Fritz W. Köhler

Translated from the German by Helgard Niewisch, D.V.M.

Consulting Editor: Matthew M. Vriends, Ph.D.

D0981720

BARRON'S

First English language edition published in 1986 by Barron's Educational Series, Inc.

© 1985 by Gräfe und Unzer GmbH, München, West Germany

The title of the German book is *Zwerghühner*

All inquires should be addressed to:
Barron's Educational Series, Inc.
250 Wireless Boulevard
Hauppauge, New York 11788

International Standard Book No. 0-8120-3687-5

Library of Congress Catalog Card No. 86-10936

Library of Congress Cataloging-in-Publication Data

Fritzsche, Helga
    Bantams: husbandry and care, diseases, and breeding.
        Translation of: Zwerghühner.
        Includes index.
        1. Bantams.   I. Title.
SF489.B2F7513   1986   636.5'871   86-10936
ISBN 0-8120-3687-5

Printed in Hong Kong

19 18 17 16 15 14 13 12 11

Front cover: Bantam with feathered legs, Porcelain male.
Back cover: above left: Amrock, Barred, female; above right: Sulmtaler, mother hen with chicks; below left: Holland White-Crested, male with two females; below right: Sebright, Golden, male.
Inside Front Cover. mixed party of Bantams.
Inside Back Cover: Cochin, male.

Photographs
Buchholz: page 10 above left, center left, below left, back cover above left, below right; Gröger: page 10 center right; Kahn: back cover above right; Lehmann: page 56 below; Reinhardt: inside front cover; Scherz: page 9 below; Wolters: page 27, page 45, page 46; Wothe: front cover, page 9 above left, above right, page 10 above right, below right, page 28, page 55, page 56 above left, above right, inside back cover, back cover below left.

Contents

Preface 4

Considerations Before the Purchase 5
Are Bantams Right for You? 5
Bantams and Other House Pets 5
Planning for Your Vacation 6

Purchase and Familiarization 7
Where to Get Bantams 7
How to Recognize Healthy Chickens 7
Home Transport and Initial Care 8
Getting to Know Each Other 8

Husbandry and Care 11
The Right Place for the Coop 11
The Chicken Coop 11
Hygiene—Thorough Sanitation and Spring-
  Cleaning 15
The Free-Ranging Run 16
The Fenced Run 16
Runs for Special Requirements 17
Hen House and Chick Pen 17
The Chicken Household 18
Temperature Requirements for Bantams 21
How to Carry Bantams 22
Preventing Accidents 22

Nutrition 23
Food Intake and Digestion 23
The Right Food 23
Rules for Feeding 23
Food and Nutrition for Chicks 24
Food for Young Bantams 25
Food for Adult Bantams 26
Food Rations and Drinking-Water Requirements
  26

When Bantams Get Sick 29
How to Prevent Sickness 29
The Annual Molting 30
First-Aid Treatments 30
The Most Common Poultry Diseases 31
A Chart of the Most Important Diseases 32
Internal Parasites (Endoparasites) 33
External Parasites (Ectoparasites) 34
Disinfection and Sanitation 35

Breeding 36
Considerations before Breeding 36
Prerequisites for Breeding Purebred Bantams 36
The First Egg—Production Capacity 37
Pairing and Brooding 37
Breeding and Fertilization 37
Broodiness 38
Setting or Not Setting? 38
Artificial Incubation 39
Fertile Eggs 39
Husbandry Chores Before and During Setting 41
The Hen at Work During Setting 42
Hatching of the Chicks 43
Is Help Needed? 43
The Growing Chicks 44
Leg Bands and Grouping 49

Understanding Bantams 50
Ancestors and Relatives of Our Chickens 50
Domestication 50
Social Behavior 51
The Behavior of Hens 52
The Behavior of Roosters 53
Courting and Breeding 53
Care of the Plumage 54
Dust-Bathing 57
Sensory Abilities 57
Sound and Body Language 58
Learning Abilities 60

Bantams from Around the World 61
Choosing the Best Strain 61
Killing and Butchering a Chicken 62
Original Bantam Breeds 62
Bantam Varieties: Facts and Figures 64
Bantamized Large Breeds 66

Index 71

Preface

Bantams are among the oldest known domestic animals. Marco Polo described silky black-skinned chickens, domesticated 4,000 years ago, as "fur-feathered" animals. Breeds like Chabos and Cochins followed about 1,000 years ago. Apart from those breeds and a series of other "dwarfs," there are now many new and magnificently colored varieties from which to choose. I have owned a "family" of Bantam Cochins for many years. These three tame, golden-feathered "feather puffs" love to be petted; they accept hand-held feed, and they come when I call them—unless they have something more important to do.

There are many reasons why someone would like to keep Bantams or Banties. You may dream of those great-tasting "natural" eggs, or you may belong to the group to which I belong—those who just enjoy having beautifully colored tame animals around. And then there are others, who are driven by the ambitious goal of breeding—they are usually members of breeder associations.

This book describes genuine Bantams and dwarfed varieties of regular chickens. Their varying requirements and characteristics are clearly described. Specific details for each breed will help you choose body weights, egg-laying capacity, housing needs, flight height, general temperament, and behavioral patterns during breeding and toward the caretaker. More than 30 color photos show the colorful splendor of Bantams. Drawings are added to illustrate helpful hints for your homemade constructions. Of course, you will find included all necessary details on correct husbandry and care of Bantams. There is a list of recommended considerations before you purchase any animals; and there are helpful pointers on housing, feeding, health-maintenance, breeding, and showing of Bantams.

I have evaluated and added much of my personal experience with my own Bantam facilities as well as the basic knowledge in chicken care which I acquired while working on a large farm. None of my experiences, though, would be sufficient to cover the variety of special requirements that Bantam breeds necessitate. For much of that particular information I must here thank the experienced breeders who allowed me access to their facilities, flocks, and knowledge, and also the presidents of specialty clubs who supplied me with the many details for each breed. Since there is not enough space to thank everyone by name, I thank a small group in the name of all who helped: E. Willig from the Zuchtbuch Bayern (Bavarian Breeder Standards); R. Moeckel; J. Stockhansen; W. Schmidt; and the families Kammermeier and K. H. Stadler.

I owe a special thanks to Professor Dr. J. Kosters (Institute for Poultry Diseases, University of Munich), who advised me on the chapter on diseases, and to H. Diepolder, who supplied me with necessary veterinary medical literature. My heartfelt thanks go to the photographers, Konrad Wothe and Joseph Walters, for their outstanding color photography, and to Fritz W. Köhler for his lively illustrations. And now, I wish you as much enjoyment with the Banties of your choice as we have with our Cochin family!

Helga Fritzsche

4

Considerations Before the Purchase

Are Bantams Right for You?

There are a number of considerations that should be made before you go ahead with your purchase of Bantams. They concern the various aspects of housing, care, and husbandry. If you have positive answers to all the questions, and you have solutions to any problem indicated, then I can advise you to start your Bantam project.

• Do you want to own Banties for economic purposes or for your own enjoyment in keeping these animals? You can only make the right choice of breeds (see page 64) after you have answered this question in your mind.

• While livestock animals must be kept as carefully as pet animals, it is important to keep in mind the fact that Bantams kept for economic purposes will be butchered relatively early in life, while pet birds can live up to 14 years. Will you be able to do the butchering chores, or do you know someone who has assured you they will do it correctly for you? Food animals have the same right to humane treatment as pet animals.

• High-quality, healthy Bantams of defined breeds are not free! The price usually reflects the type of breed, color, and popularity. Chickens live in groups and, therefore, to start with, your minimum number should be one rooster and two hens.

• You can build the coop if you are handy with tools (see page 11). Even when you build it yourself, though, there is some cost for the material to assure durability and good insulation. It is more expensive, of course, to purchase kits which you can assemble yourself.

• Bantams cannot live on food scraps alone. They require mixed grains, calcium, and trace elements. During the winter months costs are increased by the addition of greens and vitamin supplements. I assume that your Bantams would have daily access to grasses, cabbage, lettuce, and other greens during the summer. On page 26 you can find suggestions on how to keep costs low during the winter months.

• Will you have sufficient time to clean the coop three times each week? I clean our coop daily. The run needs to be cleaned twice weekly. This kind of regular, thorough sanitation is the only way to your Banties' well-being; it prevents diseases, and it prevents neighbors from complaining about malodorous conditions or flies.

• Are you willing to spend about $10 to $15 twice yearly for fecal examinations by a laboratory (see page 29)? Are you prepared to take an animal to a veterinarian or to buy veterinary medications—and to apply them reliably as instructed?

• Chickens need to be tended twice daily. Will you have a person ready to substitute for you when you have reason to be absent for more than eight or ten hours?

• Do you understand that roosters can be stopped by "the Law" from crowing? Therefore, have you made friendly inquiries in your neighborhood to get a rooster accepted in the community? Remember that a well-insulated coop is the best protection against a noisy rooster (see page 11).

Bantams and Other House Pets

Dogs: Bantams can forage freely in the yard only under the condition that your dog is fully obedient and that the dog's sense of territory and protection can be geared toward

Considerations Before the Purchase

the birds. If this is not the case with your dog, you must expect the dog's hunting instincts to be unpredictable. Once the chickens start screaming and fluttering, a dog will be increasingly motivated to pursue and potentially bite or kill. Therefore, you must consider a fence to keep peace. Chickens are instinctively afraid of dogs, and they must be given time to adjust to even the most placid canine pet.

Cats: Cats take a devilish delight in scaring chickens by stalking them from any given hiding place. They pounce into action and enjoy the screeching and fluttering of the chickens during a short chase. Cats don't present a real danger to adult Banties and only rarely to very small animals when the cat in question is more than normally used to hunting in the wild. However, chicks and young birds are truly defenseless and must be watched for about three months to assess the real danger from the cat. While a mother hen will be prepared for death-defying attacks to protect her chicks from dogs or cats, remember that an untrained, disobedient dog and any cat are faster than any protective mother hen. In any case, it is advisable to keep hens with chicks in an area that is protected on the sides as well as overhead (see page 18). For your young birds, you must weigh the conditions for your particular home. And setting hens must be protected from marauding cats and playful dogs so that they don't get scared off their nests. If that happens repeatedly, it can jeopardize the hatching success.

Guinea Pigs and Rabbits: When these pets are free to roam in the yard, they risk being attacked and injured by Bantams.

Turtles: Any pets of this group should also be kept apart from chickens, since curiosity may provoke pecking and potential injury.

Planning for Your Vacation

You cannot take chickens with you on your travels. During your absence you will need a reliable person who will take care of the chores twice a day and on time. The person can either live in your home or come in just to take care of the animals. The morning chores include opening the coop and letting the chickens get out to scratch; cleaning the coop and the feed and water containers; and preparing fresh food and supplying fresh water. In the evening it is most important to lock up the coop after all birds are accounted for.

It is strongly recommended that your Banties be familiar with your substitute caretaker. These chickens are quite frightened of strangers and they may retain more than normal apprehensions. Instruct your helper with a detailed list and, before you leave, have a "dress rehearsal" so that you can verify the completeness of your instructions.

Needless to mention, you must prepare sufficient amounts of feeds, supplements, and bedding materials. During the winter months all chores are a little more complicated, because the chickens stay inside the coop most of the time, which makes the daily cleaning duties even more important. Droppings must be removed regularly and meticulously; fresh greens must be provided; and the temperature has to be controlled reliably. All of these details must be included in your list of instructions.

Purchase and Familiarization

Where to Get Bantams

Bantam fanciers sell specific Bantam breeds. You can find addresses through your local Poultry Association. A variety of journals and magazines (see page 72 for addresses) have advertisers for many breeds, and specialty magazines publish articles of information. An advertisement mentioning the sale of certain chickens with the numbers 1–2 as prefix means "1 rooster, 2 hens"; 1–0 means "1 rooster"; 0–1 means "1 hen"; and 1–1 means "1 rooster and 1 hen." If you do not find your particular choice locally, you should contact the specialty associations for the breeds you are looking for. Whenever you inquire in writing, remember to include a self-addressed stamped envelope. Most members of local or regional poultry-breeder associations are unpaid honorary officials with mostly full-time regular professions to attend to. If the breeders you

Conscientious mother hen (shown here a Chabo hen) points out to her chicks what food is and how to pick it.

choose are close enough, you should go there in person and see how and where the Bantams of your choice are kept.

How to Recognize Healthy Chickens

In general, you can be confident that breeders as well as private owners of fancy chickens have and offer healthy animals for sale. However, to add a touch of extra care and knowledge to your considerations, here is a list of signs of good health in chickens:
• Smooth, shiny, and full plumage.
• Intensely colored red comb and wattles (this need not be true for setting hens and hens with brood).
• Alert and shiny eyes.
• Relatively firm, well-formed droppings with an occasional dropping that is darkly colored, smells very strong, and contains no hard particles in it. This type of excrement is formed and voided from the appendix. The feathers around the vent must be clean. Healthy Banties are:
• Active and curious, yet they do not get flustered when they need to be handled by an experienced person.
• Busily picking and scratching for food, and actively dusting and preening their plummage.
• Free of ectoparasites like mites, fleas, or ticks.
Make sure to ask the seller about previous fecal examinations and antiparasitic treatments. Remember that such diagnosis should be performed twice yearly (see page 29).

Purchase and Familiarization

Home Transport and Initial Care

There are commercially available transport baskets made specifically for Bantam chickens. They have divisions inside the container into which single birds fit, so that they are protected from each other and from deliberate or involuntary injuries. These containers have openings to supply sufficient air for breathing.

If you already own a cat-carrier, you can use it to transport up to three or four Banties, as long as these birds know each other and have stayed together previously. You should group them by size or age. Place newspaper on the floor of the carrying container, and cover it with some shavings or sawdust in order to absorb all moisture from the droppings. While fresh air to breathe is most important for these chickens, it is equally important that drafts be avoided. If you place the Banties in your car, test the airflow by opening a window and starting a slow drive with the ventilation on. If your vehicle has a section where the floor is heated, you must avoid that section in order to prevent overheating with ensuing cardiovascular collapse.

If you have a long trip and the weather is hot, plan frequent stops, at least every two hours, and offer your bird passengers some tepid water or camomile tea, which you bring along in a thermos. Remember to have all car doors shut and windows rolled up because a nervous chicken can just flutter up and out and away, and that can lead to bad injuries. As soon as you arrive at home, place the animals in the previously fully prepared coop, where fresh litter, food, and water are waiting. This is where they should be left alone and quiet to allow them to get used to their environment and to rest from the stress of transportation. If the new Banties are additions to your stock, you must keep the stock stringently separated from the new animals (see page 29).

Getting to Know Each Other

The day following their arrival, begin the process of acquainting the birds with you. Rule number one is to remain quiet and friendly at all times. Love and affection is given through the chickens' stomachs as much as with anyone else—that is to say, you should start by offering food from your hand. Lower yourself to a crouch while you talk to them quietly, so that they are less frightened. With just a little patience you may be successful from the start. As soon as one bird starts picking from your hand, however gingerly, the others will soon follow. If you are not in luck, repeat this on the evening of the same day, the following morning, and so on. During these periods of personally relating to each bird, you will get to know their particular characteristics one by one. This is reinforced during the daily cleaning chores, so that you know them quickly well enough to notice changes when they occur (see page 32). As soon as the Banties pick from your hand, they will also be tame enough to be lifted and carried. Most chickens retain some degree of flight reflex, but it is usually quite reduced. Once in your arm, all Banties enjoy being petted on the head, neck, and cheeks.

Above left: Crowing Feather-Legged Bantam, male. Above right: Bantam Holland White-Crested rooster in typical courting stance. Below: Two roosters in attack position.

8

Husbandry and Care

The Right Place for the Coop

Chickens require light, warmth, and shelter from wind and drafts. The coop should be constructed with an east-southeastern exposure for the front, including the window, door, and chicken doors to the run. Hedge, shrubs, or bushes should be placed toward the north-northeast and in a western location to protect the coop from winds. Despite their love of warmth, chickens tolerate heat poorly, since they have no sweat glands to allow perspiration. For noon summer heat you must plan to provide access to light shade for them. Planting a tree which keeps its foliage long into fall or winter would be a good idea. It is best to get advice from forestry specialists in your area before planting to avoid a situation where there will be puddles and mud all over the run each time it rains. Avoid placing the coop on heavy soil with a high underground water table. It is desirable to have an area about 6 feet (2 m) wide around the coop which is covered with gravel or with stone or brick steps to walk on. Where the coop is placed within the run, it is advantageous to plan direct access from the path to the coop.

The Chicken Coop

Large structures usually require permits. Sometimes you can use an existing structure—a shed, barn, or stable—to place your coop. In this case you will need to make alterations but you won't need a permit.

For all other kinds of structures the regulations change by states and counties, and you should familiarize yourself with the regulations before you plan any construction.

The Correct Size

The minimum space for two Bantam hens and one rooster is 16 square feet (1.5 m²) per Bantam and a minimum of approximately 35 cubic feet (1 m³) of air (see drawing page 14). With a coop this size, keeping the birds in a light, temperature-controlled basement during the winter months is recommended. Cover the basement floor with good litter, perches, and all other accessories. This move will allow the birds a larger area to move about in during the cold season. If you have or build a larger coop 18 to 27 square feet (2–2.5 m²), there is the advantage of better mobility for the birds during inclement weather, but it has the disadvantage of being difficult to keep warm. A compromise solution to this problem is raising the roosting perches, approximately 2.7 feet (0.80 m) above the floor space with its litter. Additional insulation for the sleeping quarters is essential. You can also put a sliding-door separation between the two areas to create warmer quarters. The sliding divider would have to be closed as soon as all chickens roost to sleep—which is as early as 5 P.M. in winter. A third alternative is to place a comfortably large box inside the coop into which the birds can retreat for the night.

Bantam varieties of large chickens. Above left: East-Friesian Moeven female in front, male in the back. Above right: Salmon Faverolle, male. Center left: New Hampshire, male. Center right: Italian, male with females. Below left: Amrock, speckled hen. Below right: Brahma, male.

Husbandry and Care

Foundations

Foundations are essential for all solid structures, and they are recommended for most wooden coops, also. A foundation should be as deep as regional frost intensity requires, which can be as deep as 3 feet (approximately 1 m) into the ground. Where the soil is soft, the foundation must be about 2 to 4 inches wider along the baseline. The width is determined by the thickness of the wall. Heavy walls require approximately 9.5 to 14.5 inches (24–37 cm) and wooden walls or light materials 9.5 inches (24 cm). The foundation should extend up to 1 foot (about 20 to 30 cm) above ground, and must be level along that line. The correct mixture for this foundation is one part cement to eight parts gravel. To offset rising moisture, it is necessary to cover the surface of the foundation with tar paper. The sheets of tar paper should overlap at least 4 inches (10 cm).

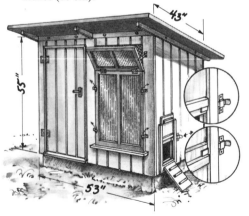

Walk-in coop, assembled from prefabricated parts. The hinged window opening is secured by chicken wire. Inserts show details of the safety closure, open and shut, to prevent wild marauders from entering.

Walls

Solid buildings should be constructed with bricks, cinder blocks, or concrete blocks. Avoid building materials that permit absorption of moisture, which would have a very bad effect on the health of your chickens. Chemically treated wood is the most suitable building material for small coops. Assembly kits are usually made from wood (see Addresses, page 72). Mini-coops can be put together from plywood pieces. Both plywood and particle board can be cut to size at the time of purchase, which is a great saving in time and trouble!

Surface Treatment and Insulation

Treatment of wood and other surfaces should be done only with chemical compounds that are not toxic to the animals. A compound with antifungal agents is good for humid areas. Clear varnish is also good. Everything should be treated or painted before it is assembled and, of course, all surfaces must be absolutely dry before animals are allowed access. There should no longer be any odor from the chosen coating.

Wooden structures should be built with double walls that have a 1½-inch (4 cm) insulation layer between them. All Bantams need warmer coop temperatures than large chickens, even though not all varieties of Banties are equally susceptible to colds.

Flooring and Roofing

Small coops, as described above, can be built either with plywood or hardwood floors. Insulation must be doubled in this case, and the boards should be especially carefully pretreated. Coating with a resin or varnish is indispensable.

Solid buildings should have brick or concrete floors and, like the foundation, they should be covered with insulating tar paper. Grouting of brick floors should be done with cement-mix grout.

Our little wooden coop is completely hinged on all joining surfaces, so that we can get in even from the top. All surfaces are made from the same material and have the same insulation all around. The hinged roof-lid allows us to clean through the top—and to lift out the Banties.

The roof surface is covered with thick roofing tar paper as protection against heavy rains. The roof is slightly inclined, to allow water to run off, and it overhangs at the front wall to protect it from downpours.

Windows and Doors

Chickens need a lot of light. Therefore, you should plan to use about one-fifth of the wall space as window area. Windows, like doors and ramp openings, must shut tightly when closed to prevent drafts. Bantams are very sensitive to drafts, as was pointed out earlier. About one-third of the upper window area should be hinged to be opened in warm weather and during warm nights. Cover the opening with chicken wire to prevent wild rodents from entering. Do not use window screens; they do not permit enough ventilation! (see page 14).

A regular door, about 6 feet high and 2 to 3 feet wide (190 cm high; 90–100 cm wide) is a great advantage when you have a coop or building large enough. If the door opens against an adjoining wall, it is easy to place a latch to secure it when it is open. Do not forget a solid lock! The door threshold should be slightly aboveground and should have a board at the bottom, about 10 inches (25 cm) high, to prevent the chickens from scratching the litter out through the door. Soundproofing is a good idea as a friendly gesture toward your neighbors. I would suggest double-glass windows and double-panel wooden doors (see Ventilation, page 14).

Depending on the Bantam breeds you plan to keep, the doors should be about 10 to 12 inches (25–30 cm) wide, and the same measurement high. It is advisable to place the doors about 6 to 8 inches (15–20 cm) above the littered floor area. If the opening to the run is not elevated, you must place a board across the inside lower part to prevent the litter from being pushed outside. The ramp down into the run should be hinged and function as a fully closing door. A sliding closure is also acceptable. In windy regions, you should plan a small wind porch just at the ramp opening.

During the first few weeks the chicks need extra warmth; even on warm days they return, repeatedly, to the warming plumage of their mother.

Husbandry and Care

Ventilation

Chickens need a great deal of fresh air, and they are very sensitive to warm, humid conditions. Three Banties need a minimum of 35 cubic feet (1 m^3) air space and well-designed ventilation. If the coop is not cleaned daily, the air quickly accumulates carbon dioxide and ammonia. This condition leads to upper respiratory disease, as well as to conjunctival inflammation. If you keep the coop meticulously clean, you need only a simple ventilation set-up which can be regulated by a sliding control mechanism as shown in the drawing on this page. In larger coops (as on page 11) there should be a window which can be opened either fully or partially. Another possibility is ventilation ducts which must also be secured by meshed wire at the inside of the coop. Never open doors, windows, or other openings on opposite sides of the coop simultaneously! (Watch out for drafts!) Instead, frequent airing is desirable.

Heating and Lighting

Under emergency conditions, Bantams will tolerate temperatures around 32°F (0°C) for just a few hours (see page 21, Correct Temperatures), but certainly not for any extended time. Therefore, no coop should be without some access to electricity. This may be needed for auxiliary thermostat-controlled heater and/or for a water heater to prevent drinking water from freezing. If you want to keep any of the breeds that require extended growth periods, and that start setting in December (e.g., Phoenix varieties), or some varieties that start laying during the cold winter months, then you must heat the coop to about 60°F (15°C), and, in addition, provide lighting. You can set a lighting timer to provide about 14 hours of light for these breeds. Light intensity should be kept at about 10 to 20 watts for each 65 square feet (6 m^2). Bright lighting is never indicated. More important is the regularity of the light cycle until natural outside lighting equals the required time period. If you interrupt or stop the regular lighting period, you will encounter reduced and irregular egg laying, decreased brooding inclination, potential health disturbances, and a decline in roosters' breeding activities. The negative effects will be most serious for both old and very young birds. If you are a beginner, you should not start by raising chicks during the winter months. When this becomes necessary, you will need an infrared lamp. The bulb must be covered by a protective grid to prevent direct touch.

Small coop for one Banty family. For ventilation you can build a hinged window or a ventilation ruler, which is pushed sideways to open or close vent openings in the wall. The little folding ramp closes tightly and is locked by a simple latch (as in the insert).

Husbandry and Care

Perches

Perches are made to size according to the feet of the particular breeds you will have. They are usually about 1½ to 2 inches wide and about 1 inch thick (4–5 cm wide; 3 cm thick) at most, and rounded at the top. As the drawing on this page shows, this type of perch gives Banties the best relaxed roosting position because it provides extra support for their breastbone while they sleep.

Four adult Banties require about 3 feet (1 m) perch length. Less will cause fighting. With this in mind, you must also have all perches at the same height.

Dropping pits (enclosures that hold the droppings as they accumulate) under all perches may be left out for small coops as long as sanitation is excellent. If you would like to use a pit, construct it with removable wire-mesh covers; use 15- or 16-gauge wire in a 1 × ½-inch rectangular mesh. It might be possible that the welded wire will need support from beneath with a few 1 × 2-inch cross-braces, obviously depending on the dimensions of the frame.

Those Banties that don't fly much or that don't fly high should have perches built not more than about 15 inches (about 40 cm) high. One foot (30 cm) is as high as Chabos Banties will appreciate. Higher perches may lead to injuries from jumping; liver injuries, for example, have been reported. There should be 6 to 8 inches (15–20 cm) between the dropping pit and the perches for small breeds, and 8 to 10 inches (20–25 cm) for others. If you have Banties with long tails, you must raise the height accordingly so that their beautiful tails won't touch the droppings.

Litter

Shavings from chemically untreated wood is the most suitable litter material. It is quite inexpensive. Shredded straw is good, also, but it does not absorb odors and wetness as well as wood products do. Oak shavings are toxic and not to be used. Peat mixtures and sawdust are not suitable either, because they are high in dust content, which presents a problem for the respiratory system of the chickens. A layer of 12 to 16 inches (30–40 cm) of litter has proven in our experience a very workable amount of floor covering.

Hygiene—Thorough Sanitation and Spring-Cleaning

Ideally, droppings and messy litter should be removed every day, but not less than every 2 to 3 days. At the same time the perches should get a quick, moist wiping off. Once you have established this routine, you will understand that it is far better than cleaning the heavily soiled coop thoroughly every other week or so. Litter need only be completely changed once each month.

The major cleaning is done twice annually, preferably on a warm day both in spring and at the beginning of fall. All of the litter must be removed and all parts and accessories of the coop washed and scrubbed thoroughly with hot soapy water, then dried. Don't use any chemicals; just basic soap is best. Wash the perches separately from the other accessories. If you can get a safe, nontoxic disinfectant containing an antiparasitic medication, use it on all surfaces after they are washed.

Husbandry and Care

The Free-Ranging Run

As with all animals, Banties do well when they are kept as close to their natural requirements as possible. They appreciate plenty of space to forage in, plenty of fresh air, unhurried time for scratching, picking, dust-bathing, or resting in the sunshine or shade.

The ideal home for a run is a fruit-tree orchard on grassland. Here, the chickens can find all their hearts desire in grass, leaves, insects, worms, snails, caterpillars, etc., and their scratching won't do any harm. This kind of a run is also much more "interesting" for them than commercial pelleted chicken scratch. Of course, orchard life has a dangerous side, too, as it gives access to wild animals, cats, and dogs—all of whom can destroy small Bantams.

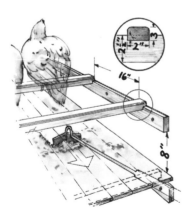

Home-made perches. The distance between perch and dropping pit is adjusted for each breed according to the size of the Banties. Long-tailed breeds require correspondingly more height.

The Fenced Run

Maybe you are going to choose one or two breeds of Banties that are not feather-footed but instead love to fly and fly high. Well, those are not bound to honor your walls or fences; they will seek your neighbor's garden—at least during their first year of growing up—and they will love to roost in trees from where you may have to shake them down each night!

To keep these birds at home, you will need a fenced run, and, for the highest-flying varieties, you will need an aviary-style run with the top covered by wire mesh.

Banties love to move around—and they need the exercise to stay healthy and active. Three animals need a minimum of 485 square feet (45 m²) floor area in the run. Small runs encourage otherwise less flight-active birds to escape. This is a natural reaction to satisfy natural requirements. If you can afford the space, plan on twice the minimum run area. This will help you prevent accumulation of ecto- and endoparasites—Coccidiosis, especially (see page 31). It is a good idea to divide a good-sized run into two parts, which are used alternately. When one side is used up, you dig it under, fertilize it, and seed it with mixed grasses for the next occupancy by your chickens.

There are various greens that grow fast and are good for your birds, depending on your climate and ground. Your local feed store and nurseries can give you the best advice. If you are close to agricultural schools, you can get first-class information there. Your best source for *free* information, advice, and pamphlets is the Agricultural Extension Service or Cooperative Extension Service, United States Department of Agriculture—look in the phone book under your county government.

Runs for Special Requirements

If you plan to have Bantam breeds with heavy or delicately feathered feet, or with long beautiful tails, you should be prepared to keep them on a manicured lawn, or, if they scratch deep, you will need a run with about 8 to 10 inches (20–25 cm) of sand, which must be kept clean all the time. Should you plan on having show birds, the feathers have to be kept in absolutely perfect condition. Some breeds need not only to be kept dry from above, but they also need to keep their feet dry. For such breeds you will have to plan a covered part—about one-third of the run. The most suitable roof material is light-transparent greenhouse cover. Under no condition should you use glass, because the splinters of a single broken glass panel can turn the entire run into a useless area.

Here, again, the highest standards of sanitation must prevail! Lawns are best hosed off; sand must be replaced from time to time. The lawn must be dry before you let the birds back on it.

Breeds living on sand require daily supplements of greens apart from their scratch, calcium, and trace element rations.

Hen House and Chick Pen

Brooding hens must be left quiet and undisturbed. They prefer to brood where they are used to laying their eggs—where they feel safe—an instinctive behavioral pattern. During the first week after the chicks have hatched, you may do best keeping them in the coop. We place our hens during that time in large moving cartons with meshed wire covers. Each box is provided with shavings for litter, with a nesting box, and with food and water. Since the space in these boxes is very limited, I do take the hen out into the yard while the chicks are feeding. They enjoy their usual feed in their familiar run. I have to take them separately, though, because otherwise brooding hens will fight.

If you have a large coop, you are better off subdividing the space to create separate brooding areas. Remember to keep unfriendly brooding hens out of sight of each other. They can get so enraged that they will step on their chicks and kill them.

If the weather permits, you should allow the chicks to be outside, at least temporarily, starting when they are about one week old. The area must be dry, temperatures around 68°F (20°C), and there must be no wind. Now you need a portable ground pen for the chicks and a brooder box in it for the hen. It should be in a sunny place, but it must offer shelter and shade. The box must be weatherproofed. Page 21 shows an example of such a set-up. We chose 16 square feet (1.5 m²) as an area sufficiently large, but small enough for the chicks to slip under their mother's plumage frequently for warmth, and not be exhausted from too much running about. Not all hens are instinctively careful with their chicks, and they do not necessarily encourage their chicks to keep warm or to move before they sit down. In order to permit the hens and their chicks to be outside most of the day, you should cover the pen overnight with plastic or foil in order to keep the whole area dry for the next morning.

When the temperatures outside stay above 59°F (15°C) at night, you can leave mother and chicks in their outdoor enclosure. It is most important, though, to have the brood box at least 1 to 2 inches off the ground, so that the chicks don't get moisture and cold drafts through the floor at night.

The Chicken Household

Well-designed accessories of good quality are not only recommended to ease your chores, but they also serve to keep chickens happy and in good health.

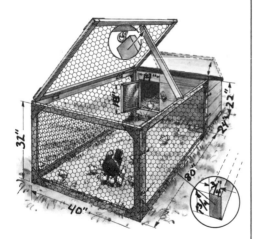

This caged-in run protects the chicks and their mother from cats and other predators.

Feed Bowls

For a small flock of three or four chickens, you need only a large glazed ceramic bowl—about 6 to 7 inches (15–17 cm) wide and about 2½ inches (6 cm) high—with a rim that is turned slightly inward (see page 25). This type of bowl is easily cleaned, stands solidly, especially if the base is a little wider than the rim, and it helps to keep most of the scratch inside the container. Plastic containers are not a good idea, because they are lightweight and tip easily.

For more than a few chickens, it is better to have commercially available chicken feeders. These are suitable for chicks as well as for adult Bantams. They are available in various lengths, starting at about 1 foot (30 cm). Elevating these feeders slightly is recommended to keep the feed clean. Bantam chicks are best fed for the first few days from "feeder boards," which are also commercially available. If you have only a few chicks, you can serve them their meal from plastic lids like those of margarine dishes or freezer containers. There must be enough feeding area to allow all chicks to pick at the same time! For eight chicks you need at least 8 × 8 inches (20 × 20 cm). As early as one week after hatching, the chicks are agile enough to feed themselves from the regular chick-feeder. If you like keeping the feeder outdoors, you can buy one that is covered. This becomes a requirement if you do not feed inside the coop or if you don't have another lowered feeder space. If your chickens are kept inside the coop, you will find galvanized, suspension baskets most suitable for feeding greens. Place the hanging baskets at a height that requires the animals to stretch their necks to get to their beloved greens. This promotes good exercise and alleviates boredom. All feeders must be removed weekly and washed thoroughly with hot soapy water, then rinsed and dried. The containers should be checked mornings and nights, and they should be cleaned without delay if they are soiled with droppings.

Baskets are suitable feeders for greens inside the coop. This method prevents badly soiled floors.

Waterers

Several types of waterers are available commercially. If you have only very few Banties, you may use an inverted waterer as shown on page 25. This type can store up to a pint (1/2 l) of water. They are usually made from plastic, and they must be washed thoroughly and regularly with hot soapy water. New chicks need only the plate filled with the empty reservoir inverted above.

If you want to feed sour milk or yogurt products, you should use glazed ceramic containers or stainless-steel automatic waterers. Other materials will be damaged by the acidity and the dissolved chemicals may be harmful for your animals. Important: Elevate waterers over grates and over sand to prevent the soil from getting wet and the water from getting dirt in it. Suspended automatic waterers are preferable in all cases, as they help to prevent stagnation and contamination of the water. Algae on the containers and coccidia growth around wet water plates are best avoided. Water lines to the automatic waterers should be underground below the frost line, and, in cold climates, plastic pipes should not be used, since they tend to burst easily when the water freezes. Stationary waterers and plates must be cleaned and filled with fresh water daily.

Nesting Boxes and Nests

All hens like to lay their eggs in a nest that is in a quiet, semi-darkened, well-prepared place with good, clean nesting material. The hen takes about two hours from sitting to leaving the nest. Therefore, we gave a nest to each of our hens. This stopped the noisy complaining when they all wanted to lay at the same time.

Individual nests are usually homemade (as in the drawing below). Such nests can also be used for brooding. Most hens prefer to brood in the same place where they are used to laying eggs.

If you want to breed (see page 36) purebred chickens, you must know exactly which egg originated from which hen. Where there are only a few hens, it is easy to tell characteristics for each. Gretel, one of our hens, for example, lays round cream-colored eggs, while Emma, the other hen, lays brownish and elongated eggs.

If your hens' eggs are not different from one another, or if you have many laying hens, then you must use nests with egg traps. These can also be constructed at home (see drawing on opposite page).

The Dust Bath

Dusting is designed to condition the plumage, and at the same time it is an enjoyable pastime for all chickens (see page 57). If you do not have a naturally suitable area in your yard or run, you can build a dusting pen quite easily. Use wooden boards about 1 inch thick (24 mm), 6 to 8 inches (15–20 cm) high, and up to 2 feet long and wide (50–60 cm), as shown on the drawing at the right. The dust pen must be in a spot that is protected from rain in summer, and it should be indoors during the cold months. The best dust-bath composition is a combination of fine, dry earth and clean, dry sand. This mixture should form a layer of at least 5 to 7 inches (13–18 cm). Droppings must be removed frequently, and the sand should be changed every few weeks.

Handy Accessories

Carrying baskets: There are commercially designed carriers available that are designed specifically for Bantam chickens.
Nail clippers: Where chickens are kept on lawns or on soft, sandy ground cover, their nails do not wear off as fast as they grow, so that you need clippers to trim them from time to time.

Thermometer: Each coop should have a thermometer, preferably a hygro-thermometer, which measures temperature and humidity. The device should be wire covered for safety, and it should be placed at the height of chicken roosts and nests.
Incubators, Brooders: These pieces of equipment are only required for large-scale breeders, and for the rare case when a desired breed refuses to set and a foster hen is not available (see page 61).
Infrared Lamp: This accessory is useful for early-season breeders, but also for sick chickens with colds. The use of infrared lamps in connection with sick animals should get a veterinarian's go-ahead.
Thermostatic-Controlled Heater: Small accessory heaters, inexpensive and safe, are a very good idea, as they serve as automatic watchmen during cold spells. When you purchase this heating device, you must get a model that is right for the floor space of your coop. It should also indicate that it may be used safely in a humid environment.

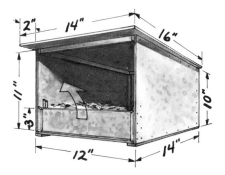

Home-made nesting box. The board at the bottom front lifts out in order to facilitate easy cleaning.

Husbandry and Care

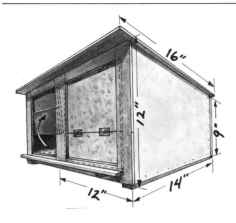

Nesting box with trapping mechanism. Once the hen has entered, she cannot open the flip-panel from the inside.

Temperature Requirements for Bantams

During the first week of life, chicks require an even temperature of about 90°F (32°C). For every additional week of age, the temperature can be lowered by 4°F (2°C). This temperature must be kept accurately for artificially-hatched chicks. Naturally-hatched chicks should stay inside the coop with their mother in a confined space of not more than 16 square feet (1.5 m²) and an ambient temperature of not less than 60°F (15°C). If there is more space provided, you run the risk of the mother hen running about too much and neglecting her chicks' need for warming underneath her plumage. Young birds, up to 6 weeks of age, require an ambient temperature of about 57°F to 71°F (14°–22°C) and thereafter of about 59°F to 64°F (15°–18°C) until 16 weeks of age,

when they have developed their full plumage.

Adult Banties like temperatures ranging from 57°F to 71°F (14°–22°C), but they are also happy at higher temperatures as long as they have access to shade and sufficient air. The coop must have excellent vetilation (see Ventilation, page 14).

Winter temperatures of 32°F (0°C) can be tolerated only for a short time, and only if there are no drafts or moisture. When the environment is humid indoors as well as outdoors, there is a risk of circulatory disease if temperatures are kept as low as 43°F (6°C). Ambient temperature during winter inside the coop should be a minimum of 21°F (10°C) for mere survival, but that is too low for breeding and egg-laying activities. The thermostatically-controlled heater is the best accessory to prevent problems of this nature.

You must be very careful when you allow your chickens to run outside on sunny, cold days. Frostbite on combs, wattles, or feet can

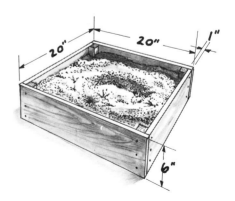

Dusting pen for Banties. The contents of sand and soil must be kept clean by regular removal of droppings.

Husbandry and Care

persist as permanent damage with poor affects on their general health and resistance. (See Temperatures for Sick Chickens, page 29).

How to Carry Bantams

There are a number of veterinarians and farmers, as well as breeders, who will pick up chickens by the roots of their wings. While this does not cause injuries, it has been proven that it is painful and that chickens do not like it and return the favor by withholding trust and affection. The method by which the birds are held by their legs is acceptable only for specific veterinary-medical treatments or examinations. This method should only be used as restraint for short procedures; for any extended purpose, such as carrying, the held-leg method is nothing but cruelty and lack of humane concern.

As long as the birds are still shy and unused to being held, I recommend that you pick them up slowly, by carefully reaching over the middle of the wing, down the side, and under the breastbone. Lift and hold the Bantam close to your body on your arm. The wings must be held down smoothly. This is the easiest, safest method for beginners.

Preventing Accidents

Coop windows must be screened from the inside with meshed wire to keep out wild marauders.

Electrical bulbs must be shielded by wire from direct touch, and electrical cords must be out of reach for pecking as well as scratching. Chickens can get fatally ill when the coop is wet, cold, or poorly ventilated. Overheating is just as dangerous to their health.

Tame Bantams follow their keeper around the yard, whether you are mowing the lawn or doing other chores. This is how they run underfoot or risk getting hurt by equipment. With this type bird you should be extra alert concerning their whereabouts—or better, lock them up while the environment is unsafe for them. All kinds of poisons to combat insects, weeds, snails, rats, or anything else can cause serious disease, even death, if eaten by your Bantams. Resist all temptations to use these chemicals. There are snail treatments available without poison; weeds can be pulled out; and other uninvited guests can be prevented by ecological gardening. Should you run into a situation where nothing else but toxic chemicals will do the job, then you must plan to keep the birds inside a secured run for several weeks.

Fertilizers are usually dissolved after two or three days if they are thoroughly dug under and if the ground is well soaked.

Chickens must never be left to roam in places where cars or motor bikes are parked, cleaned, or repaired. Birds get violently ill from the consumption of even minute amounts of gasoline, engine oil, or polish. Even in diluted concentrations, as in puddles, the toxicity is still strong enough to cause diarrhea, gastrointestinal ulcers, lethargy, weight loss—and potentially worse. Ingestion of any amount of antifreeze is always fatal.

Nutrition

Food Intake and Digestion

Chickens have no teeth and, therefore, swallow their food whole. The food stops first in the crop, which bulges after a meal; from there, it passes to the preventriculus, a glandular stomach that predigests the food; and then into the gizzard, the muscular stomach where the food is ground up for digestion. This grinding is performed by hardened mucosal ridges and muscular action. The grit in the chicken feed assists this grinding process and explains the necessity for small stones and sand in chicken scratch. The mechanical breakdown of the food is supplemented by enzymes and bile secretions, until all ingested material is processed sufficiently to get all possible nutrients absorbed for the needs of all body tissues and fluids. The undigested materials, unsuitable for further use, are passed through the intestines where excrement is formed into droppings that are voided through the vent. Chickens have paired sets of appendices in which the major breakdown of cellulose occurs by means of specific bacterial components. This digestive process becomes visible as light-colored, foul-smelling, soft droppings. Food that is particularly hard to digest, and excessive amounts of food are stored in the crop for some time. Saliva and some regurgitated gastric juices go to work on predigestion, before the food is passed along into the stomach.

The Right Food

Our ancestral chickens fed on worms, seeds, insects, snails, and greens. Their food contained all necessary nutrients: carbohydrates, fats, plant- and animal-protein, minerals and vitamins. Our domesticated versions of those chickens have the same nutrient needs, and it is good if you allow them to forage for some of their food.

When you consistently offer them a variety of scratch, animal protein, minerals, and greens, the chickens make up their own correct nutritional diet plan. There is a potential problem in leaving out one or the other nutrient compounds for some time. Once you add it, the chickens may overeat the food they missed until then.

Rules for Feeding

Drinking water should be fresh, clean, and not too cold. Do not use pelleted, milled, or packaged feeds after the expiration date. Food should be stored in a cool, dry, well-ventilated space protected from excessive dust and from vermin.

Once food products get soaked or soiled, you should throw them away. Clean the feed and water containers daily.

A good caretaker recognizes the importance of close observation as it affects consistency or changes in the amount of food that is consumed. If you find no trace of food left mornings and evenings, increase the amount. If you find leftovers regularly, decrease accordingly. Soon you will know the right amount. Remember that you should expect more food to be consumed during cold weather in order to replenish energy losses.

If you want to change the type of feed, you must do so slowly and consistently to

Nutrition

avoid digestive problems. You can use approximately three-quarters of the familiar food for four days, then mix half and half for the four following days, then proceed to one-fourth the amount of the previous food before you are ready to give the full feed ration in the new form. If, while you are doing this, your Banties eat poorly, stretch the time out to an even slower pace.

Owners of only a few birds can afford to spoil their chickens a little by obliging them with their favorite foods. Needless to say, you should never be tempted to give your chickens peoples' foods that are salted, spiced, or heavily sweetened, no matter how tasty they are for humans.

Food and Nutrition for Chicks

During the first 24 hours after hatching, the chicks consume the remainder of the yolk. At this time, it is critical to keep the chicks quiet and warm.

As soon as they get hungry, they will be seen picking aimlessly around in the straw. That is the sign to feed them. Remember, though, that chicks hatch up to two days apart, so that they are not all ready to be fed at the same time. Checking is necessary.

Chicks should drink fresh, clean, tepid water before they are first fed. Get them used to the chick-waterer from the start. Sometimes you may need to dip the beak of each little chick carefully into the water, and watch that they actually swallow with their little heads leaning backward.

Basic Ration: Chicks must be started on a special high-protein ration with minerals for baby chicks. There are various ways to ac-

complish the right feeding. Mostly, it is convenient to purchase a complete baby-chick feed that is commercially available from several manufacturers. Some types of chick feed must be ground to smaller particle size for chicks up to three weeks of age. You can do that with a coffee grinder. It is strongly advisable to feed chicks up to eight to twelve weeks of age with feeds that contain antibiotics and coccidiostats.

If you are willing to pay a little more, especially if you have only a few birds, I highly recommend that you buy the food that is especially prepared for the raising of pheasants. This food comes in two compositions, one for the first three weeks of age, the second for chicks from three to nine weeks old. After that, you mix the food with oatmeal. I like to prepare my own mixture, and this has worked well so far. I mix about one-half pheasant food with finely mixed chick-feed and oatmeal. After two weeks, I add some pheasant scratch or canary-feed mix.

Greens: You start feeding greens from the fourth day on. Tender leaves of nettles, dandelion, chickweed, garden cress, also a little chives and grass—all finely chopped. Why don't you just leave a corner of your yard unweeded, so that these greens can grow there. Of course, you can just as easily seed and grow a nice mixture in nursery flats. Suitable mixtures are available in feed stores and nurseries as well as through catalogs and magazine advertising. Trim the larger plants frequently to encourage new growth of tender young leaves.

Starting at about two weeks of age you can also feed chopped cauliflower leaves (no cabbage, though!), watercress, chives,

24

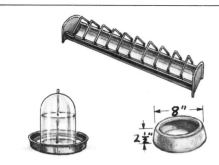

Chick-feeder; ceramic food bowl; chick-waterer, suitable for chicks and adult Banties alike.

and the greens of garlic and onions which appear to have a healthy cleansing effect on the intestinal tract.

Food Supplements: Bird gravel will be an essential requirement starting at two weeks. It should be offered in a separate clean dish where it will be available at all times. I also add a dash of a mixture of minerals and vitamins daily. Make sure you check the expiration date on these products.

Feeding Schedule: During the first week, the chicks need to be fed every two or two and one-half hours. Water and feed are offered for ten minutes each time. If you stay with the chicks, you will notice any abnormal behavior such as loss of appetite, diarrhea, etc. These are alarming signals! I like to feed the youngest chicks every two hours from 6 A.M. to 4 P.M. Their little crops are filled this way—and they can last through the night until their morning feeding. If you are a late riser, you can make the schedule to 7 A.M. to 5 P.M. However, that's as much stretching as can be tolerated. Chickens are daytime animals!

Starting with the second week, you can stretch feeding intervals to three hours. The last meal will be offered at 5 P.M.

Starting with the third week, you can leave the food out all the time, as long as there is adequate space, and as long as the hen does not scratch the food in all directions. If you have good chick-feeders and chick-waterers, all is well (see page 18). The last mealtime now is around 6 P.M.

Food for Young Bantams

Basic Scratch: From the ninth week on, young bantam pullets and cockerels should be fed food specifically prepared for the young birds. Starting at twelve weeks, grains and grit are mixed in. If you mix it yourself, make sure that wheat is not the sole grain, since it has insufficient protein content for chickens and could cause severe health problems. I like to feed the second-phase pheasant food and to that I add mixed grains. By the twentieth or twenty-fourth week, the change to adult scratch should be completed.

Protein: Animal-derived protein is an essential daily food requirement for your chickens. In addition to the protein that is contained in the commercial pheasant scratch, I supplement daily—from the ninth week on—with one tablespoon of canned cat food, which is enough for eight young birds. Soured milk, yogurt, or low-fat cottage cheese are also good.

Greens and Supplements: Just as chicks do, the young growing birds need both. Now to the list of greens for chicks you can add spinach and everything that grows in the yard or run. Grit and graveled sand are mandatory. Vitamin preparations with minerals and crumbled cuttlebone are also essential.

Nutrition

Food for Adult Bantams

Basic Scratch: Adult birds receive greens just like the young animals. During the winter months, we put some of the scratch in the clean litter.

In addition to this, you can add in some wild birdseed mixture, because it has a higher fat content. A little less than one teaspoonful per bird is about right. You can add fat, also, by mixing the scratch with some salad oil or castor oil—just enough to moisten the grains. This mixture must be prepared fresh every day. Leftovers must be discarded. Fats serve as a good energy supply in cold weather.

Protein: The same is used as was indicated for young birds. Just increase the amounts accordingly. Milk products must be of room temperature if you feed them during the winter.

Greens: Adult Banties like the same greens as young Banties do. Today you can buy most of them fresh throughout winter. Supply greens in suspended baskets. Oats, wheat, and barley are very suitable seeds for runs that need fresh-grown greens. During the winter months, you can grow greens from these grains by using nursery flats filled with earth. You can put the whole flat down for the chickens to pick from. Wait until the green sprouts are about 2 inches high. If you prefer, you can pull out the green with its roots and chop it up for feeding. Good temperatures for sprouting start at 59°F (15°C). Seeding is most successful in your house or in a little greenhouse. High-quality hay from clover and wild greens is a welcome addition to greens fed in winter. Chop it very fine, give it in small amounts, and keep it dry.

Food Supplements: Commercially available vitamin and mineral supplements are as important for adults as for youngsters. During the winter months, during brooding periods and molting seasons, you should also add vitamins once per week to the drinking water. Follow instructions to the letter, and discard water that is more than 24 hours old.

Food Rations and Drinking-Water Requirements

The amount of food that is required varies among breeds, varieties, ages, stage of maturity, molting, and environmental temperatures. The general method and place where your Bantams are kept is another factor that influences the amount of food intake. You just cannot tell unless you observe your flock personally (see page 24). A general rule about the amount of drinking water is that the volume of water should be about twice as much as the total dry food. Of course, there will be variations according to the outside temperature; there will be an increase in water consumption if the food is high in proteins; and a lowered consumption when greens are provided in abundance. Keep the drinking water tepid in winter; this is best accomplished in a temperature-controlled coop or by way of an automatic waterer that is thermostatically heated (see page 20).

Ancestral Bantams and Crested Bantams. Above left: Feather-legged Bantam, Buff, female. Above right: Chabo, Black with White (Butschi). Center left: Holland, White-Crested Blue, female. Center right: Bearded d'Anvers, Partridge, male. Below left: Ruhlaer Kauler, Black with White, female. Below right: German Bantam, female, original color.

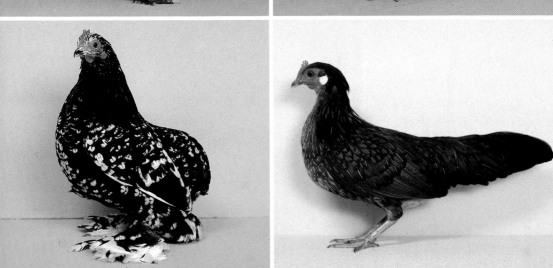

When Bantams Get Sick

How to Prevent Sickness

Careful husbandry practices are the surest prevention of diseases. Here are the most pertinent points on that subject:
• Most infectious diseases are transmitted through the fecal excrements. Therefore, it is essential that the sanitation of the chicken coop have top priority, and that feeders and water containers are cleaned daily. Moisture enhances conditions for the growth of germs. You should try to keep the overall environment dry but not dusty.
• High-nutritional food quality enhances the general physical resistance of Bantams during the winter months.
• Frostbite or death by feezing are caused only through incorrect housing. While some Bantam breeds have adapted well from their original warm Asian habitat to western cold seasons, they are certainly not ready for involuntary experiments on tolerance to cold air and frost. Those breeds must be kept in a temperature-controlled coop as soon as temperatures range around 32°F (0°C), and when the weather is cool and wet. For any weak or sick animals, you must provide temperatures of about 68°F (20°C).
• When the feather coats of chickens get soaked, they are just as stressed as through hunger, heat, or dehydration, and any one of these stress factors will make the chickens more susceptible to diseases. Therefore you should provide your animals with a safe, dry

Bantam families. Above: Yokohama male (center) with hens and chicks, at the left of the rooster is a Padua chick. Below: Holland White-Crested, male and females.

area that is always accessible to them for protection from rain or other unclement conditions. Of course, this does not substitute for your watchful eyes, since these animals are not necessarily "reasonable" enough to go to the shelter. Should your Bantams be drenched, you must place them in a room of at least 68°F (20°C), and leave them in dry straw bedding for several hours before allowing them back into the open stable area. The use of a blow-dryer is not recommended because the animals are frightened by the noise.
• Parasites and diseases are frequently brought in from the outside by the addition of new stock. Therefore, you must adhere strictly to a five-week quarantine period for newly acquired animals. During this time, you must watch them carefully and you should get a fecal lab test done to diagnose and treat parasites.
• Fecal tests are recommended twice annually, preferably in January and June or July. You can mix the fecal samples of several chickens, since the infectious nature of parasites will affect all equally, and all chickens that were in contact with each other would have to be treated if one were found affected. However, if you observe one animal with particular symptoms, take a separate fecal sample from that animal and mark it clearly. Place the fecal sample in a piece of aluminum foil, then into a tightly sealed jar or metal container for mailing. Should the result show parasitic infestation, the veterinarian will prescribe the appropriate treatment. If you observe your animals well, they will tell you whether any tests are necessary in addition to the biannual ones.

When Bantams Get Sick

The Annual Molting

Don't panic when you observe increased loss of feathers toward the end of summer: molting is not a disease! Feathers turn into dead, insensitive tissues after they have finished their growth and purpose. They are shed and must be replaced. This process is called molting. An adult chicken molts annually in late summer or early fall. It takes several weeks to replace all of the smallest feathers on the body and head. The new feathers push up right behind the old ones, so that the process never leaves real bald spots on the animal. The large feathers on wings and tail are replaced slowly in a specific sequence over an extended time. This process allows the chickens to keep their ability to fly even during the molt. Quite naturally, the molting process takes up extra energy and, therefore, places the chicken in a more susceptible health condition. However, if care and nutrition are generally well attended to there is no reason to worry about decreases. (Hens do not lay eggs during molting season; roosters do not breed.) Young chickens molt twice during the first six months of their lives: first, the down feathers are replaced, then the first young feathers are replaced by the adult feathers. Antiparasitic treatments should not be done during molting, since that could interfere with healthy feather formation.

First-Aid Treatments

In the case of minor health problems, you can try to deal with the treatment yourself.

• At the first signs of diarrheal onset, use tetracycline or an anti-coccidial medication (coccidiostat) according to instructions (available from feed stores or veterinarians) and offer some lukewarm camomile tea.
• In case of minor cold symptoms, warm the housing temperature 64°F to 68°F (18° or 20°C), and assure yourself that the area is dry and draft-free (yet has enough ventilation). Sometimes an infrared lamp is helpful.
• Small injuries can be cleaned with Phisohex: Swab with 3% peroxide, dab dry with *clean* cloth, and finish with any human wound spray or with Furacin powder.

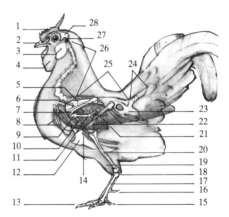

Anatomy of the Bantam: 1. Comb   2. Beak
3. Cheek-wattle   4. Chin-wattle   5. Humerus (upper arm)   6. Scapula (covered)   7. Radius and Ulna (lower arm)   8. Clavicle (wishbone)
9. Metacarpus   10. Thumb bone   11. Wing bone
12. Keel   13. Front toes   14. Breastbone
15. Back toe   16. Spur   17. Shank bone
18. Hock joint   19. Thigh with hock joint
20. Tibia (lower leg)   21. Ribs   22. Femur (upper leg)   23. Pelvic bones   24. Tail vertebral bones
25. Lumbar vertebral bones   26. Neck bones
27. Ear   28. Skull

When Bantams Get Sick

• Unless you notice a marked improvement within one to two days, you should contact a veterinarian! With up to three or four chickens, you can go to the veterinary clinic, but if you have more, the veterinarian has to be asked to make a house call.

• Any time there is abnormal fecal color or consistency, a sample should be tested as soon as possible in order to start treatment immediately.

• Medication prescribed by the veterinarian must be administered in exactly the recommended dosage and exactly following the time schedule to prevent side effects.

The Most Common Poultry Diseases

Coccidiosis

Infection always occurs through the ingestion of infested fecal matter in unsanitary or humid pens. Coccidiosis can be a more or less serious disease depending on the accompanying circumstances or stress factors, such as excessive heat or cold; deficiencies; crowding; or molting.

Symptoms: Weakness, ruffed feathers, diarrhea; soiled vent.

Prevention: Good husbandry practices; addition of coccidiostatic agents (chemicals to inhibit the growth and multiplication of coccidia) to feeds of growing chickens (especially in large productions).

Treatment: Prescription drugs such as sulfonamides and other coccidiostatic medications. Observe prescribed dosages and administration schedules. Supplement food with vitamin B inbetween treatments.

Infectious Hepatitis

This infectious agent occurs in chickens and many other birds. Chickens pick it up at an early stage, when it is passed on with fecal ingestion. When the infection turns into disease, it is mostly due to wrong husbandry.

Symptoms: Weakness and apathy; atrophy of the comb; or diarrhea.

Prevention: Optimal husbandry; minimal stress condition.

Treatment: Veterinary medical-prescription drugs administered with feed or water; eventually high-dosage streptomycin by injection.

Marek's Disease

This is a reportable viral disease which occurs rarely, but is to be reckoned with.

Symptoms: Young chickens usually become lame in one leg and/or wing. Adult animals may show a variety of disturbances of motion—wings or legs; however, these symptoms may disappear after just a few days.

Prevention: Artificial incubation and hatching of the eggs from affected parent chickens with subsequent immunization of one-day-old chicks. These will remain healthy. Kill the affected animals, disinfect the coop and run thoroughly, and start with chicks.

Treatment: None.

Poultry Typhoid Fever:
White Diarrhea of Chicks

The germs that cause this disease survive in the earth, straw bedding, and dust for months. Chicks are frequently infected by adult animals who show no external symptoms. The chicks are most susceptible during their first few days of life. Older adult ani-

A Chart of the Most Important Diseases

Symptom	Potential Causes
Puffed-up feathers; chicks move closely together.	Environmental. Temperature is too low; fever (normal body temperature 106.7°F (41.5°C).
Lowered appetite; refusal to take food or water.	Foul-tasting or spoiled food or water; initial stage of an infectious disease; separation from the imprinted lead person; separation from stablemates or change in environment.
Unseasonal molting.	Recovery phase after a serious disease.
Rough, dulled feathers.	Poor nutrition; incorrect husbandry; disease; parasites; other stress factors.
Feather picking; cannibalism.	Boredom due to space restriction; poor, unbalanced nutrition.
Coughing.	Dusty straw bedding; increased ammonia due to poor sanitation; cold, humid environment; drafts; drenched feathers; extended periods of temperature below 32°F (0°C).
Nose-cold with nasal mucus around the neck feathers; tearing eyes causing an owl's-head expression.	Cold and other causes as for coughing; infectious respiratory disease.
Breathing with an open beak.	Environmental temperature too high; lack of shade; fever.
Severe respiratory disease with extended neck ("tail-breathing"—tail moves with every forced breath).	High fever or overheated environment.

In case of the following symptoms you must consult a veterinarian:

Clearly audible, rasping breathing sounds.	Inflammation or irritation of the throat or trachea by tracheal worms.
Lameness with associated pain.	Fracture, sprain, or contusion.
Lameness without signs of pain.	Marek's Disease.
Head turning back; uncoordinated motion; trembling.	Salmonellosis; vitamin E deficiency; spoiled food; parasites.
Formed fecal matter in urine puddles.	Kidney disease.
Fresh blood in feces.	Bleeding rectum or terminal colon.
Reddish-brown colored fecal matter with mucus.	Gastro-intestinal bleeding.
Grassy-green feces.	Liver disease.
Very soft or fluid diarrhea (not to be confused with excrements from the cecum).	Hepatitis; Coccidiosis; Toxoplasmosis; Mycotoxin ingestion via spoiled moldy food.
White-colored diarrhea.	Bacillary White diarrhea (no treatment).
Restlessness; continual scratching and preening with beak and talons; pale coloring of face and appendages.	Flea and mite infestation.
Fear of the chicken coop.	Infestation of housing quarters with red mites.

When Bantams Get Sick

mals will succumb to the disease only when their general immune-response is lowered.
Symptoms: Poor ratio of hatching chicks; whitish diarrhea in young chicks; breathing distress, and high mortality. Affected adult birds show weakness, lethargy, and weight loss during a protracted siege of disease.
Prevention: New birds and parent birds should be examined for pathogens. Affected birds should be killed without delay—either butcher it for consumption or have it euthanized humanely by the veterinarian for disposal of the carcass.
Treatment: Once flocks of chickens are infected, there is no cure for the animals. Antibiotics or sulfa drugs can only alleviate some of the disease symptoms.

Infectious Catarrh: "Rup"

This is predominantly a bacterial infection of older birds rather than of young animals.
Symptoms: Sticking collar feathers; owl-headed look; unpleasant sweet-smelling odor; seriously encrusted nasal orifices with dry mucosal surfaces, including the tongue. The disease lasts for two to three weeks.
Prevention: Quarantine for newly acquired birds; thorough disinfection of coop and run.
Treatment: Antibiotics by prescription and vitamin A therapy. The damaged mucosal covering of the tongue, no matter how bad it may appear, will normalize unaided during the endstage of the disease.

Tuberculosis

This bacterial infection affects mainly weak birds. It is a reportable disease.
Symptoms: Weight loss; rough feather coat; lameness in advanced cases.

Prevention: Optimal husbandry and care; highest sanitary standards; complete, balanced nutrition.
Treatment: No treatment is feasible because of high costs, excessive duration of treatment, and uncertainty of results.

Internal Parasites (Endoparasites)

Despite highest husbandry standards, there are worm parasites that find their way in any flock of chickens. The responsible carriers are typical food animals for Bantams such as snails, earthworms, or beetles. This is one of the major reasons why biannual fecal testing is highly recommended.
Roundworms: 1½ to 4 inches (4–10 cm) long, found in the small intestine. *Hookworms:* 4½ to 5½ inches (11–13 cm) long, in the appendix. *Cecal worm:* ½ to 2 inches (1–5 cm) long; in crop, pharynx, cecum, and small bowels. *Tracheal worms:* ¼ to ¾ inch (0.5–1.8 cm), in the trachea. Affected birds sound hoarse. *Tapeworms:* various types and various lengths, in the small intestines.

When chicks are heavily infested with coccidia, they are so weakened by diarrhea that most of them will die.

When Bantams Get Sick

Treatment: The veterinarian prescribes a suitable treatment for specific diagnosed worm parasites.

External Parasites (Ectoparasites)

Chickens in optimally sanitary housing conditions are not usually affected by ectoparasites. However, it is recommended that you examine your flock from time to time for any potential invader. Newly acquired animals must especially be examined carefully, and also the feathers of hooded breeds.

Red Bird Mites
Mites are minute specks that are difficult to see (0.3–0.7 mm). They have 4 long pairs of legs and multiply quickly. During the day this parasite stays in dark hidden places of the coop from where it leaves at night to crawl onto the chickens to feed on blood.
Prevention: Thorough sanitation. When you are doing the major cleaning chores, remember to clean all possible nooks and niches where mites can hide.
Treatment: Repeated treatments with medicated powder and repeated disinfection of the coop after the birds are treated. Avoid eyes and beak when dusting the animals.

Feather Mites
These mites are visible at close inspection (1–5 mm) with a distinct head section. They feed on scales of feathers and skin. They cause continued itching and disturb the chickens to such extent that they will lose weight quickly, and egg laying decreases rapidly. These mites are always on the bird.

Fleas
Fleas are visible; they are light brown (2–3.5 mm) with a laterally flattened body. They suck blood, cause itching and disturb the birds.
Prevention: Pay extra attention to nesting boxes, especially of setting hens. Change the nest material frequently, at least every two to three weeks.
Treatment: As for mites.

Scaly Legs Mites
Minutely small specks of 0.2–0.5 mm with four stumplike legs. This mite bears live offspring; it lives on the legs and toes of the birds, where it sucks blood.
Treatment: Apply baby oil or salad oil to feet and legs, up to the shanks. These mites will suffocate through contact with oil. You must repeat this treatment weekly. Usually the problem will be solved within six weeks.

For the administration of tablets or pills, place the medication on the back of the tongue, hold the beak closed, and wait for the bird to swallow.

When Bantams Get Sick

Ticks

These parasites are oval-shaped, 3–11 mm long and they only spend their feeding time on the chicken. When they are full of blood, they fall off.

Treatment: Dab some oil on the tick, wait ten minutes, then carefully pull the tick off. The head must be removed.

Flies

The housefly, about 3–10 mm long, as well as all other flies which feed on dirt, carcasses, and all kinds of spoiled organic matter, are signs of a dirty, insufficiently sanitized chicken coop. These flies tyrannize the chickens and, what's worse, they transmit diseases. When your chickens have small lesions, like injuries from fights to establish a pecking order, flies can infect them by laying eggs or larvae in their wounds.

Prevention: Keep the coop and run areas clean. Try to prevent unnecessary fighting.

Treatment: Place fly-strips in places where the chickens cannot reach them. Clean wounds with Phisohex or with a 3% peroxide solution; dab dry with clean cloth or tissue and apply simple wound powder. Gaping wounds must be treated by a veterinarian.

Important: Never treat ectoparasites and endoparasites simultaneously. Such treatment could have side effects so serious that they could cause death. Treat the worst condition first, wait at least three to five days, then treat the second condition.

Disinfection and Sanitation

Once your flock has experienced a course of disease or parasite infestation, a thorough cleaning procedure is called for. First, remove as many items as possible from the coop, and proceed to clean everything by scrubbing and scraping away old manure with hot, soapy water. Subsequently, you must disinfect all surfaces. Never mix detergents and disinfectants, because mixing will eliminate their effectiveness.

There are various good disinfectants available at grocery stores, through your veterinarian or janitorial supply house.

Make sure you follow instructions for dilutions meticulously. Use scrub brushes, spray bottles, and tree-sprayers, depending on the size of the coop facilities. Allow the coop to dry well before you allow its residents back into their dwelling.

Left: Chicken legs affected by "scaly legs." Right: Healthy leg for comparison.

Breeding

Considerations before Breeding

The term ''breeding'' can be used in a variety of ways: Allowing a hen to set and raise her chickens—without control of the genetic specifications—is a way of breeding for multiplication; while breeders who use purebred varieties use the term strictly to mean the continuation or creation of a specific breed—or characteristic of a genetic line. The same differentiation is valid when eggs are hatched in an incubator.

Before you start any breeding, you should consider the requirements for space which are mandatory for hens with chicks. Mother and offspring must be kept separate from the others in the flock (see page 17). If you do not have the space for more Banties but would like to enjoy the experience of breeding, you must plan to have takers for your 10- to 16-week-old Banties when they have grown to young adults. The planned owners should be kind and animal-loving, but you are responsible for their chicken-keeping preparations being adequate. If all of this seems too much trouble, you are better off letting a broody hen set on an empty nest for about three weeks. Then clear the nest away. The hen will complain for a day or two and then get back to normal life. Another alternative is to allow a broody hen to set for about three or four days, after which time, take away the nest and place the hen in another enclosure. This method is usually enough to change a broody hen's mind.

Prerequisites for Breeding Purebred Bantams

The *Standard* refers to the *Standard of Perfection*, a book published by the American Poultry Association, which describes and defines characteristics of color, size, etc., of each breed and variety of chicken. Each country conforms to the accepted *Standard* of that country.

To start breeding purebred Banties, you must group breeder animals according to breed, size, shape, colony, egg-laying capacity, and temperament, exactly according to the outline of the *Standard*.

Once you decide to breed Banties, you are strongly advised to join a local poultry-breeders association. If there is a specialty-breeders association in your area, you should definitely join it, too. Local organizations are very important for you because they help with much information, contacts, addresses, and other details that will save you time, trouble, and mistakes.

You cannot get rich from breeding pure-bred Banties. There are always expenses for food, housing, and accessories, and, in addition, you must add costs for the purchase of "new bloodlines." There are roosters or hens that are not your own breeding flocks' offspring, and they are necessary to prevent unwanted genetic problems from inbreeding.

Show prizes are quite infrequent. Decorations, ribbons, and trophies are reserved for true champions! Preparing the birds for a show takes up very much time and attention to detail. It is most important that, as a beginner, you discuss the matter in depth with an experienced show-breeder. To show your chickens you must reserve your place well in advance, pay the show fees, and arrange for transport and local housing. It is to your advantage to transport and tend your animals personally both before and during the show. This is much less stressful for the birds than exposing them to unfamiliar caretakers. After a show the birds should be quarantined for at least a few days to prevent potential transmission of a cold or another unrecognized disease.

The First Egg—Production Capacity

Hens start laying eggs at about five to six months of age, depending on the breed. Should this age fall during the cold winter months, you will have to wait even longer.

Most hens lay eggs constantly for about four to six years, before their egg production decreases. Many healthy, strong hens continue past that age, and raise healthy, strong chickens as well. However, at seven years their biological aging process begins.

The first egg is usually of normal size, but is produced with a thinner shell than the later ones. After our hen Emma laid her first soft-shelled egg, I found only small remains, because the three chickens found the new "thing" so interesting that they picked most of it by the time I found out.

We produced a nesting box in a hurry and provided it for the hens by the end of the same day. You can use hay and chopped straw as nest materials. Food must now include daily supplements of calcium and mineral mixtures to strengthen the egg-shell production. This will prevent further egg breakage.

The degree of egg-laying productivity depends on a variety of factors, such as breed, parents, type of housing, feed, husbandry, season and, of course, the general health of the hen. There are no eggs produced during brooding and molting periods. There are, also, less tangible factors that lead to reduced egg-laying: a change of owner, keeper, or environment is stressful and can cause a hen to decrease or even stop laying eggs for the time it takes to get adjusted.

Pairing and Brooding

April/May are the Spring months that naturally generate pairing and brooding instincts. The same behavior can be generated artificially in winter by optimizing and controlling the ambient temperature to 60°F ($+15$°C), and by extending lighting time to 14 hours each day (see page 14). All other factors can remain unchanged. Hens require about two to three weeks to adjust to optimal egg-laying conditions, while it takes roosters more than five weeks to get in the mood for breeding, and to be successful in their activities. Breeding in winter is not for beginners! Without any efforts of your own, natural laying will start in February, and you can count on fertilized eggs by March or April.

Breeding and Fertilization

A rooster has no penis. Sperm is transferred by extrusion of the vent to the outside and is received by the hen in her vent.

It takes about 28 hours from ovulation to egg-laying. Since fertilization takes place

Breeding

Signs of Egg-Laying Activities

Body Section	positive	negative
Head-Appendages	Swollen; well-vascularized.	Shrunken, pale.
Ventral Pubic-Bone Area	Protruding; soft; skin delicate; skin can easily be lifted over pubic-bone area.	Flat; tight; skin is tough.
Vent	Large; moist; pale.	Puckered; dry; pink.

right at the beginning of this process, you have to plan a two-day delay before you count on fertilized eggs. Unused sperm cells remain healthy and viable for about ten days, so that all following eggs can be fertilized during this time.

Roosters can breed successfully for about six years, but they are usually allowed to breed for two years only. If the rooster does not like a hen, he will not breed with her. Fertilization results are frequently poor if you have more than two or three hens for one rooster.

Broodiness

Some breeds have lost their broody behavior through prolonged use of artificial breeding methods. If you have a breed that is still natural, then hens will be "broody" after a certain time of laying eggs. Remember that eggs evolved for the purpose of species preservation, not for our meal tables!

You can recognize a broody hen by her characteristic sounds which change from a sing-song type "talk" to consistent "clucking" sounds, which are already the preparation for the later calling of her chicks. Hens will literally scream angrily if a rooster does not respect her obvious broody mood and goes on bothering her with unwanted attention. Even her favorite keeper will get an impatient peck with the beak or unmistakably angry discouragement for looking in on a newly setting Banty hen. Only time and long-term trusting relationships will yield an untroubled setting hen.

Setting or Not Setting?

One cannot always give in to the hen's desires. There are many reasons not to let her set—lack of friends to take the chicks is only one of them. Chickens can get broody at unwanted times, regardless of our plans or climate. Sometimes they start too late. If they are delayed in setting until the middle of May, you must have optimum husbandry conditions to succeed with healthy chickens during the following winter and to have the offspring start laying the following spring.

Setting Bantam Silkie hen in her basket. Most setting hens prefer covered nesting boxes.

Breeding

Earlier setting time is much better because the chickens will have the longest possible exposure to fresh greens; sun, warmth, and light; and outdoor scratching.

Some breeds are the exceptions to the rule, because they have longer than normal maturation requirements. These hens start clucking and setting in early January. Difficult breeds of this type are not for beginners! Here is a last appeal for consideration: Chicks create a lot of work, even if you have an experienced mother hen. The less space you have, the more work it is, because mother hens with chicks need to be kept separately from the other chickens, and they need a room that can keep temperatures between 65° to 70°F (18°–20°C). They will need this for at least four to six weeks. A separate pen is also needed (see page 37). During the first week, you must feed them every two hours; later, every three to four hours (see page 25). Daily cleaning chores cannot be cut short. When the weather permits, you must have the time to take mother and babies outside, and bring them back in as soon as it becomes damp, cool, or windy. If the weather is inclement, you must still find the time to take the mother hen out three times each day, so that she can void, dust herself, and get a rest from her babies.

If you decide not to have chicks, or if the season is getting too late, follow the advice given on page 36. If, however, you feel prepared for everything that has been pointed out, then you can give your broody hen the "go ahead" to set.

You should know that some hens will just appear broody and will leave their nests after setting only for a little while. Therefore, I advise you to put a clutch of eggs under the hen only after you are sure she is serious—after she has set steadily for two days, and after you can see that she returns to her nest shortly after each feeding.

Artificial Incubation

Rarely will you choose this method if you want only a few chicks. You will need an incubator—smaller versions are as good as larger ones—a heating plate, an infrared lamp, and a warming device for the chick-waterer. Before you buy any of the accessories, you should visit an experienced breeder and get some pertinent advice. While artificial incubation saves you some of the dramatics of a clucking mother hen, you are, in fact, missing a delightful little adventure, and, above all, you will have to spend a lot of time tending the baby chicks. I strongly advise beginners to first get experience with the natural hatching process of their hens, before they turn to artificial hatching.

Fertile Eggs

You can start collecting eggs as soon as you recognize the rooster's breeding behavior. His timing depends on light and temperature conditions. During extra-long cold winter spells you may have to wait longer, unless you prepare the coop conditions for winter breeding as described on page 38. Most eggs are laid during the morning hours. You should remove the egg as soon as possible after it is laid. The hen will unmistakably announce the event. First the egg is weighed, and the right weight for the breed is checked.

Breeding

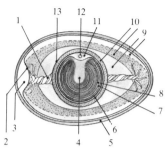

Structure of a healthy chicken egg:
1. Umbilical cord   2. Internal membrane of the shell
3. Air space   4. Embryonic yolk   5. Hard shell
6. Yolk sac membrane   7. White yolk   8. Yellow
yolk   9. Liquid albumin   10. Gelatinous albumin
11. Blasto dermal disc   12. Blastoderm (Bloom)
13. Egg membrane

If the weight is acceptable for hatching (see page 64), the egg is marked with the weight, date, and the name of the hen. Use soft pencils only to write on eggs. Ballpoint pens or other ink pens may be absorbed and can damage the egg. You may find that the pencil marking wears off during hatching, but it remains legible until the chicks hatch.

Exclude all eggs that are too light, as well as those that are misshapen. Such eggs will either not develop normally or the chicks will not be viable. Preferably, do not use dirty eggs, which should not exist in a good, clean coop with a healthy hen. Dirt may work its way through the shell in the form of infectious germs. Allow as many eggs for each hen as she can cover completely. Depending on the many breed sizes, this number can range from 8 to 12. If all eggs are fertile, you can count on an average of 75 to 100 percent hatchability.

Storing Eggs

Eggs for hatching are best stored lying flat or tilted at an angle, with the dull end up. Temperatures should be kept between 46°F to 57°F (8°–14°C), possibly in a refrigerator. The temperature must be checked daily and accurately, because the blastoderm can be damaged from 41°F (5°C) on down. Conditions that are too warm are just as bad.

Kept under the correct temperature conditions, the eggs will stay fresh enough for 14 days. It is generally accepted that the fresher the eggs are, the better. This is due to the inevitable loss of moisture that occurs during storage. Any amount of moisture loss is a direct loss to the developing chick's nutrient environment.

In order to keep the blastoderm viable, the eggs must be turned along their longitudinal axis daily. Never turn them upside down!

Once the stored eggs are too old for incubation, you can either use them for your own consumption or you can use them as test eggs for a broody hen.

Fertile and unfertile eggs

Unfortunately, one cannot recognize a fertilized egg until it is incubated. If you buy a candling box, it will allow you to distinguish fertilized eggs starting one, three, six, or seven days after incubation—depending on the quality of the device. Brown eggs take a longer time before you can identify chick embryos. Make sure that you follow instructions to the letter!

After three days, you can recognize the blastoderm (bloom) clearly in an egg held horizontally over the candling light. A healthy, developing egg will allow you to

Breeding

watch the bloom stay on the top while you slowly turn the egg around its longitudinal axis. Remember not to turn the egg upside down! Remove infertile eggs. At the time of the second candling—which should be on the 18th day—the embryo is fixed. In the meantime, you were able to determine dead egg contents and to remove them from nest or incubator. You should perform these egg examinations while the hen is out foraging, in order to prevent unnecessary stress for the setting hen.

The Developing Chick Embryo

Once eggs are fertilized they stay viable for development until the temperature is raised to start the growth of the chick embryo. Ideally, incubation requires around 100°F (about 38°C) and 60 percent humidity. The temperature needed varies for different eggs and for different equipment; for example, "still-air" or "forced-air" incubators. Follow directions exactly.

After only 24 hours of incubation, the chick embryo has formed head, eyes, and body shape. Three days later there are vessels, and the heart starts beating. Then follow lungs, liver, and bile, and at the end of one week there are skin, feathers, and the beak. The vascular circulation transports nutrients between the yolk and the embryo, and the unused end products are eliminated into a urinary cyst close to the umbilical cord. The hard eggshell provides the necessary calcium salts for the embryo. The egg shell is porous, which allows the essential exchange of oxygen with carbon dioxide.

The whole embryo is suspended inside a liquid-filled sac where all maturation takes

place until hatching. Just before hatching, the air space increases, while the now-diminished yolk is turned into the internal cavity of the chick, where it serves as nutrient provision for the 24 hours following hatching (see page 43).

Husbandry Chores Before and During Setting

Hens must be absolutely free of ectoparasites if they are to set quietly and consistently. Reassure yourself by examining your hens just before they start setting. Parasitic infestation can so weaken a bird that she cannot sufficiently warm the eggs. Check for mites, fleas, and their eggs. If you check the coop

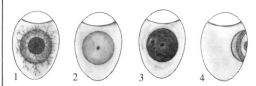

Images of developing chicks as seen over a candling box: 1. Fertilized egg   2. Unfertilized egg
3. Early-terminated development   4. Terminated, "dead" embryonic sac   5. Well-developed embryo,

14th to 15th day   6. 18th day of embryonic gestation
7. Embryonic development stopped on 10th to 11th day
8. Chick before hatching (not recognizable during candling procedure)

41

Breeding

at night, take a flashlight and check around the vent opening of the hens; that is where mites will congregate to suck blood. Act instantly with the appropriate medication (see page 34), or get your veterinarian to advise you. You should have a fecal diagnostic examination made before the laying season begins (see page 29).

The Setting Hen's Nest Box

If the nesting box is the same one the hen used for laying eggs, you must clean the box thoroughly and sanitize it before you line it with litter for setting.

A very suitable sort of nesting material is composed of a layer of shavings with a layer of chopped straw above. If the coop is large, you can place the nest box into a quiet corner there. If you have more than one setting hen, build separate portable nest pens and keep the hens far apart.

Placing the Eggs

After you remove test eggs, you should warm the chosen eggs to your body temperature before you place them in the nest. A good time to do this is the late afternoon when the hen is sleepy. Move quietly and slowly while talking in a calming and reassuring voice, and you will not run into any trouble.

Caring for the Setting Hen

Scratch should be composed of mixed grains with a lot of barley. This ration should best begin around November. Calcium, trace minerals, grit, and large-grain sand are also needed!

As soon as the hen sets, you should eliminate greens, soft foods, also canned cat food and meat. This is necessary to prevent otherwise potentially soft droppings of a hen from being eliminated into the nest while she is setting. Soiled eggs can lead to damaged, infected chick embryos. Feed and water containers must be cleaned thoroughly once or twice daily. I do this in the morning and at noon. Hold the hen gently with both hands, one under the chest, one over her back, and place her outside to feed, to void herself, and to enjoy her dust bath if the weather permits. A good sign of health now are large, firm droppings. At this time, the hen will also go about her motherhood gymnastics, fluffing and wetting her wings, running back and forth, and generally shaking herself back into good condition.

Floating Embryonated Eggs

Much egg moisture is used up during incubation, which can sometimes result in hatching difficulties. To prevent this from happening, I advise you to float the eggs on the nineteenth day of incubation. This is done as follows: While the hen is outside for her gymnastics, fill a wash basin with water at exactly 98.6°F (37°C), as measured with your thermometer. Place the eggs carefully in the water and allow them to float for exactly one minute—not more, not less. Remove them and put them, wet, back into the nest. Never replace this method by spraying water on incubating eggs. This would promote fungal growth and embryonic death.

The Hen at Work During Setting

The embryonic development of a chick (gestation) lasts three weeks. Seeing the hen

42

set cozily on her eggs may appear an idyllic sight, but in fact it is hard work: She uses much body energy warming her brood, while she skimps on her time for eating, drinking, and picking greens. Therefore, she loses weight visibly. Her plumage turns duller, and her facial appendages turn paler—all signs of physical exertion.

While she sets, the hen is turning her eggs regularly, and she also changes their location in the nest. During the first days, the hen moves the eggs several times each hour. This behavioral pattern keeps the blastoderm unattached, and it assures even warming for all eggs. It is known that the temperature difference between the top and the bottom of an egg is about 4°F (2°C). Turning the eggs gives them a chance to move from the edge of the nest to right under the hen's warmest spot, and the other way around. Many setting hens develop bare spots on their chests, which turn out to be the warmest spots for eggs to be.

Hatching of the Chicks

On the twentieth day after the egg was set, the developed chick will pip. With the help of a tiny, hardened spot on the tip of the beak, the chick breaks the membrane to the air space, which allows it to start breathing. With the ability to breathe, it commences to peep with ever-increasing sounds. The mother hen responds with a low, calming sort of clucking—which sounds a little like ventriloquist chicken talk. The peeping and clucking are loud enough to be heard by a keeper. It is always exciting to experience ''peeping eggs.'' After a quiet rest period,

the chick will use all its available force to pip by picking a hole through the hard shell at the dull end of the egg where the air space was. The tiny hole is enlarged by picking at the broken edge and turning its little body with the help of its left foot. The maneuvering is eased by leftover liquid egg white, which makes the inside slippery for turning. Before the chick can hatch, it must wait for the involution of the yolk sac through the umbilical opening, which then must be closed for hatching. Finally it will start picking a line around the egg, starting at the first hole, until the two egg halves break away. After a short breather, it struggles out of the shell, pushes up on its tiny feet, and exhaustedly, with wet down feathers, rests on its belly for a little while. But under the warm plumage of the mother hen, it quickly recovers and dries. It takes only one-half to one hour before it is strong enough to lift its head and take a few stumbling steps. At this point the chicks will frequently stick their little heads out from under mother's feathers—which is rewarded by the mother with a firm but gentle effort to push them back under her warm belly. The usual hatching takes about 12 hours from the first chirp to the fully hatched chick.

Is Help Needed?

The question arises only rarely because hatching is usually left to the mother hen who takes care of everything. The keeper should remove the eggshells left from hatched chicks so that new chicks won't get hurt by them. If, however, a chick is found that can't hatch by itself, the question of

Breeding

whether or not to help arises. Breeders consider chicks that are too weak for hatching as too weak to keep in a breeder's flock. These chicks are left to die. You can make the same decision, but you do not have to. One of my chicks looked just like its birthmates at six weeks of age—yet at birth it needed help, and even before hatching, I could see by candling that the embryo was smaller than those in all the other eggs. At hatching time, 12 hours had passed since this particular chick had started pipping and had not progressed. I cracked the shell open a tiny bit more—but stopped immediately, because I could see a drop of blood. My help had come too prematurely. A few hours later, I heard a rather vivid chirping song, and I could see the chick move quite vigorously. At this time, I removed the little rascal from the shell. I could see by the small bloody spot at the umbilical cord that the yolk had just recently been involuted. I held this miniature patient wrapped in a light, clean towel between my two hands in my lap until the down was dry and the blood had coagulated. This did not take long. Then I tucked it back under his mother's plumage. During the first day, there was a marked difference between this chick and his mates: He was a real runt, smaller and in constant need of warmth despite his good appetite, and he was quickly tired after any short outing from under the mother's safety. The condition remained for about two weeks. Fortunately, my little favorite guy was not mistreated by his family, nor was he treated as an outcast, and at six weeks of age he flew as well, ran as well, ate as well—and was generally as wicked as all the others.

The Growing Chicks

Chicks need much warmth during their first week of life. The first 24 hours of life are spent sleeping, except for an occasional awakening to announce their presence with a sleepy but happy peeping song, to which the mother responds dutifully and without delay. After only a few hours, the chicks know their mother, and they will know their keeper just after a few days of life. As soon as mother leaves for a while to eat, drink, and void herself, her absence is filled with loud, desperate, shrill peeping—the crying of the abandoned, as Konrad Lorenz described it. As soon as mother reappears, the crying turns into cheerful, contented chirping.

Once the yolk nutrients are absorbed, the chicks get hungry and need food. They begin to pick aimlessly at the litter. Water and food must then be ready to be offered on flat little boards or plastic lids (see page 24).

If your mother hen is a "reasonable" bird with good instincts, she will call her chicks, point out the water and food, show them how to pick it up, and tender her babies little morsels in her beak. This lesson is quickly successful. The chicks take the food from the mother and start picking on their own.

Some mother hens also show their chicks how to drink; however, I have not observed any specific calling sounds. If the babies don't understand the need for drinking, you will have to help them learn. Pick them up

Bantam Breeds. Above left: German, light, male. Above right: Silkie, original color, female. Center left: Modern English Game, male. Center right: Araucana, original color, male. Below left: Orpington, Buff, male. Below right: La Fleche, Black male.

Breeding

carefully, one by one, in your cupped hand, and dip each tiny beak carefully into the water (see drawing, page 48). You recognize that they are actually drinking the water when they tilt their heads back and slightly open their beaks for swallowing. Allow enough time to repeat the procedure. In order to make sure that all the little candidates got the right idea, separate the "graduates" into a carton after they have learned the lesson of drinking and keep them separate until all have learned the lesson. After two days they will no longer need your assistance. Nervous hens are often not successful in their instructions. They may start scratching wildly, causing feed, sand, and chicks to tumble about all together. Remedy: Place mother outside in the run where she can find her scratch, and feed the little ones inside by placing the food on a board or plastic lid and tapping your fingernails on that surface to make a "picking" sound. Speak quietly to them; soon, they will get the message.

Sleeping time diminishes from day to day. Often you can find chicks already on the fourth day funning about with their mother, and scratching around in the litter like "the old folks" do. The boldest ones will flutter clumsily onto their mother's back. When mother hen has had enough of the fuss she will push the adventurers back under her plumage gently, yet firmly.

Their first personal cleaning attempts can

Bantamized large breeds. Above left: Sussex, Yellow-Columbia, female. Above right: Brabanter, Golden, male. Center left: Kraaikop, Gold-Necked, male. Center right: Phoenix, Orange-Necked, male. Below left: Leghorn, female. Below right: Wyandotte, Silver, female.

be watched between the fourth and the seventh days. Balance is the key word—if you watch them tumble while they are trying to scratch their little heads. If the chicks have a mother as a teacher, they are ready to take their sand-baths properly by the time they are one week old.

Wings mature faster than the rest of the body. By the seventh day real feathers are already growing at the tips of the wings. At this time the chicks practice flying by lifting themselves up to 1 foot (30–40 cm) off the ground and landing instantly. Soon they can follow their fast-walking mother by flying and running at the same time. If the weather is warm enough, the whole family should spend as much time as possible in a protected outside run (see page 18). This will permit them optimal exercise, sun, fresh air, and access to greens which they have to learn to pick and choose. Remember to take the whole portable pen with the nest-box, feed bowls, and waterer into the outdoor area. The third week of life starts with new growth of feathers on the back and underneath the tail down. The tails look like cute little powder puffs, while the rest of the chicks look mottled and slightly ruffled. Their new feathers grow in hornlike sheaths, which are picked off and swallowed by their mother. Soon the chicks will do this for each other.

At the age of three weeks, the chicks are pretty talented fliers. They scratch and feed themselves; however, they still prefer their mother's calling and showing them where and what to pick.

New sounds of communication are now added to the happy chirp, the sorrowful cry of abandonment, and the slightly pained

Breeding

tweeting: A more or less shrill trill indicates sudden fear—the sight of a large earthworm or a fat caterpillar—or just any new threatening object. Then there is a very soft trill sound which they produce as a sign of safety and warmth when they are ready to sleep under mother's warm body. There is also a short outcry of a squeaking nature that announces little accidents like tumbling over each other or being stepped on—accidentally—by mother's foot, or even when being caught by their keeper.

Finally, the little combs start to show—all uniformly yellow at this time. Wing tips reach all the way to the end of the tail, and both the desire and ability to fly are increasing by leaps and bounds.

Nevertheless, the chicks still stay close to their mother, and while they scratch for their own food, you will find them screaming their little heads off when the mother dares to walk away by herself. When one of the chicks finds a tasty bite, it will busily put it aside—yet, not complain when that precious piece is swallowed quickly by one of the sisters or brothers. During the fourth and fifth weeks, the youngsters start looking just a bit weird—more like miniature vultures.

At four weeks and a few days of age, you can finally differentiate between males and females. Males now have larger combs which are colored pink, and the wattles at the throat and cheeks are clearly visible. The combs of pullets have not grown yet, and they are still not colored. For the chicken species, it is interesting to know that females are sex-determining, contrary to humans and mammals: The hen has the $2n + xy$ chromosome; the rooster has the xx-chromosome.

During the fifth and sixth weeks, the combs of the pullets turn fire-red. Brothers are now proving to be increasingly stronger, fresher, and bolder than sisters, but their playful fighting and quarreling lasts only a few seconds and remains entertainment. It is comical to watch sisters try to huddle under their bigger brothers when their mother is not immediately available at bedtime; unfortunately, these attempts stay unrewarded. Mother is still patiently watching over all of them and she still sleeps with her children, even warning them during the day from time to time. However, between these mothering duties, she goes about on her own. Day by day, she becomes less apprehensive of other hens, yet still avoids any contact with a male. Clucking sounds diminish further, until her prematernal singsong is back. Sisters and brothers continue to stay closely together. They learn that their mother no longer returns as soon as they cry for her. When they get sleepy—depending on the daylight time—they go to sleep by huddling closely together with brothers and sisters.

Watering a chick. Hold the chick gently, yet firmly.

Breeding

At about eight weeks of age, the youngsters are finally starting to look like miniature editions of their parents. The males do not yet have their completed tails, but the final shape is outlined, and their first plumage is fully developed. In their behavior now the youngsters resemble a schoolyard at recess time.

During the ninth week of life, the first macho males are showing off by starting to fight with each other. While these fights do not last long and do not lead to any injuries, they are actually serious and serve to establish ranking order. The strongest most vital birds are usually the winners, but they are not necessarily the best representatives of their breed, nor the maturest. The pullets are not participating in these social struggles, and they are considered taboo by their brothers. The females will establish their ranking orders a little later as young adults. Weak cocherels have to endure a few rough days during this time. They are starting to practice crowing at this time, also. The result of these vocal efforts resembles a squeaky door more than a rooster's proud crow. In between these voice practices they are still communicating in the same chirp as their sisters, adding a new melodic whistling sound to their repertory.

Most hens will leave their children at about eight weeks of age. The youngsters are doing fine without their mother, although they usually cry for a while trying to get mother to come back. The "real" plumage starts to grow at twelve weeks of age. Within four weeks it will be complete. At that time, the young fellows have achieved their father's crowing ability and the females can now

"talk" like their mothers. This is the right time to handle, carry, and pet the young birds gently and frequently, so that they will stay trusting and friendly.

Leg Bands and Grouping

Banding is usually done at the age of 12 weeks on pure breeds. It is done by placing the ring over the three front toes, then lifting the hind toe carefully but firmly, and passing the ring over it and onto the leg. Bands are available through the poultry associations.

Many breeders separate males from females between the ages of 8 to 12 weeks. This is a useful practice for large-scale breeding, for early-maturing varieties, and for the protection of the young females, as they have all been living together from the time they hatched. Our hens started laying eggs at the expected time and the male never bothered them prematurely. For Bantam fanciers, it is not considered important to feed cockerels with high-protein food, as many breeders of large males recommend.

Understanding Bantams

Ancestors and Relatives of our Chickens

Our domestic chickens date back to an ancestral wild chicken that was native to the warm regions of Asia: India, Burma, Amman, Sumatra, and Java. Domesticated chickens were brought to the western countries at different times and divided into many groups according to the geographical area where they were settled and bred. There are geographical identifications of breeds such as "Mediterranean," "European," and "Asian," which identify the places of domestication and breeding rather than the ancestral home of the chickens.

There are four basic groups of ancestral chickens: Bankiva, Sonnerath, Lafayette, and Forktail. Keeping all controversy concerning this subject in mind, the Bankiva appears to be the officially accepted ancestral chicken. This bird had the character of the game chickens, the coloring of the Italian, and the size of the original Bantams. The other ancestral breeds appear to have also had a major influence on the evolution of modern chicken breeds.

The four original breeds were similar in their life styles: The males fought for their territories during spring. The strong males would share a territorial area with up to five females. These hens would go out and search for hidden nest places; the males would help. The hens lay between five and six, and up to nine eggs. The shells are whitish or light pink in color and the eggs weigh about 1 ounce (30 g). Chicks hatch between 19 and 21 days. The mother takes care of her chicks for a few weeks and protects them from pre-

dators. The male also helps with the protection of the family by warning them of any impending danger. The chicks of these breeds are ready to fly from branch to branch at only one week; at 12 days they can follow the mother on a flight; and at 12 weeks they have changed their voice modulation to that of adults. Wild roosters crow with shrill and sharp sounds with a very short cut-off last phrase. Only the Lafayette male, originating in Sri Lanka (Ceylon), has a sonorous melodic chirp like "chick-tcho-cho-yik." Contrary to our domesticated breeds, the ancestral wild chickens change into an inconspicuous plumage after the summer molt, and their head appendages involute. Outside of the breeding season, these wild chickens live in large communities of up to 50 birds. They search for food as a group mornings and evenings, and they search in places where there is environmental protection from predators. Their flight abilities help them to escape predatory pursuit, also.

The fork-tailed progenitors of our domestic chickens are considered the most attractive ancestors. Unique among these breeds, they live in pairs. The female lays about six to ten eggs. The chicks mature slowly, males reaching breeding age in their second year of life. There are several zoos and animal parks where you can see fancy varieties of the ancestral breeds of chickens. There are only a few private fanciers who breed them.

Domestication

Ancient civilizations used chickens mainly as sacrificial animals and as entertainment in cockfighting spectacles. Cock-

Understanding Bantams

fights are, unfortunately, still not eradicated in the world—despite their ugly, inhumane nature. Although the exact development is not know, meat and eggs were used as consumer foods very early in history.

The Silkie is said to have been domesticated 4,000 years ago. Marco Polo describes it in his travel log. It arrived in China from Tibet. Chabos have been known for about 1,000 years, and Bantams have been around for a long time, also. It is known that in 1860 there were bantamized Cochins kept as court pets in the Chinese Imperial Palace garden. Domesticated chickens were already exported during the fourteenth and fifteenth centuries B.C. from China to Egypt and Persia, and from there to southern Europe. Chickens reached western Europe directly from Asia around 600 B.C. Even today you can still find South American varieties that look as strange as if they had just been taken out of an ancient Polynesian seafarer's trading baggage.

Social Behavior

Domesticated chickens, as were their progenitors, are social animals that like to live in groups. A singly kept chicken will get lonely, lethargic, and will eventually waste away. People are not suitable substitutes for chicken-mates. These birds cannot be housebroken, so that a close human-chicken relationship is not practical and is not fair to the animal. If a chicken has been kept alone with humans for a while, it will no longer be able to adjust to mates of its own species, and that, again, is an unforgivable mistake you should not make!

The Chicken Family

Banties are best kept in small families of one rooster with two or three—but not more than five—hens. One more is too many—and decidedly not feasible. On the contrary, males of many breeds are happy with only one female. My Cochins are a typical example. The problem arises, however, that a single hen is bred too often by one male, which soon exhausts the hen.

Within a family, the birds know each other very, very well. Each group member has a specific ranking order. This stringent hierarchical order is not defended by quarreling. The group holds closely together, faces potential enemies together, preens each other, and sleeps cuddled up and warming each other.

Male Fights for Ranking Order

Minor fighting starts at an early age (see page 49), and while it looks fierce, it does not usually result in injuries. The opponents rush toward each other, halt for a moment—head down, neck feathers standing on end—then jump at each other, fighting with beaks and toes until one of them flees, pursued only for a moment by the winner. This establishes who goes first and who follows second. At the teenage level, there are some rough fights to be observed! A breeder told me that the youngsters have been seen to go on fighting for a whole day. Still, none get hurt seriously in the process. If a small wound occurs, treat it conscientiously as described on page 30.

When mates of a group grow up together, and if they are of calm breeds, their ranking fights will be resolved without bloody scars, and the group will live peacefully hence-

Understanding Bantams

forth. I know of two Cochin roosters who pick and preen each other's necks regularly in greatest friendship and never overstep their social rules by approaching each other's hens. Fighting game breeds also behave peacefully when they are familiar with each other from youth on. Serious fighting occurs most frequently in groups where males are brought together at adult ages. Fights can be so serious that the winning opponent can follow the loser and finish him off to the point where the bird must be butchered. In most cases I advise that males of unfamiliar background should be separated, even if they belong to quiet, friendly breeds. If the males are left together they will try to breed the same hen, which annoys the hen who tries to escape, and that, in turn, leads to unfertilized eggs—and too much stress for all involved.

Pullet Fights

Pullets establish their ranking order with quicker and less violent fights than do their cockerel brothers. The losing female retreats and is not pursued. You may, however, observe her looking around with her head down and seemingly embarrassed. In accordance with good chicken etiquette, the female winner does not show off triumphantly; she does not push the lower-ranked male away at the feed bowl; and she does not insist on her status when the nest box is occupied.

Ranking orders among hens do have critical importance at the time of broodiness. At this time, the superior female will chase an inferior female off the nest box by beating her beak on the head of the lower-ranking hen. I am told that hens of fighting-game breeds express irritation with more vigor.

Another time of contentiousness among hens is when they are leading their chicks. Frequently, it will be the lower-ranking female attacking the higher-ranking female. While ostensibly defending her chicks, it is obvious that her anger makes her so blindly aggressive that she does not watch where she is stepping. Unfortunately, all that defending can lead to dead chicks. It is best, therefore, to prevent the entire matter by providing separate coops and runs for each family.

The Behavior of Hens

Bantam females stay in continuous closeness with their rooster and their female mates. While they are out foraging a female may go her own way, but she will not stay completely out of sight. As soon as the male calls, the hens rush toward him and joyfully accept a tender green he points out or a delicate morsel he tenders with his beak. Dusting is naturally a pleasure that is more enjoyable in company than alone. Hens also pick and preen in company, attending to each other—and especially to the rooster in their family. Hens busily and carefully pick the male's neck feathers where he cannot reach with his own beak. At night, you will see the hens roosting cuddled up to their "beloved husband" or on the floor in the straw huddled under his wings. When the male performs his courting dance, you will not discern any behavioral response. None of the females seems to encourage his mating, no matter how well he performs. The breeding act is tolerated by the female; there are no signs of pleasure. After she is bred, the hen shakes her plumage back into shape and

52

Understanding Bantams

goes on about her daily chores of scratching, foraging, and so on. Contrary to this lack of excitement, the hen responds richly to her mothering duties setting and raising her children (see page 38). At this time even the shyest females are self-assured, even bold, when they fuss with their chicks.

The Behavior of Roosters

Roosters are caring and protective heads of households and they make good fathers. In some breeds, however, instinctive behavior has been curtailed by incorrect and inattentive inbreeding methods.

Our Cochin male, for example, stays attentive and alert during foraging times, while the females walk about scratching and picking, unconcerned with their environment. The male warns his females of cats and dogs, and he chases away competitive feeding birds such as starlings or pigeons. They cannot get close to the feeders. The male learns quickly which of the four-legged creatures are acceptable, which are enemies. If they are friendly intruders, they will be announced only by a pro forma acknowledgment. If, however, they are strangers or an animal that has previously been chased away, the rooster will give a shrilly high-pitched sound of excitement, almost to the breaking point of his vocal capacity. Should the stranger approach, you should know that roosters as a rule will be the first to run.

A good male contributes not only by his watchful warning calls, but also announces good food discoveries and always lets wives and children feed first. This social arrangement makes sense biologically, because hens are hardworking and need a lot of energy to accomplish good egg production and setting. Presumably the males need less food in general because they have more body fat, despite their selfless social behavior.

Our rooster is also very friendly to his chicks. He brings their attention to suitable food morsels and picks for them. Once in a while he will pick on a chick—but never roughly. As soon as the chicks are out in the garden, he turns into a very watchful and bold defender. Social conventions of chickens require a rooster to be not only a good father but also an inflexible patriarch. He can demand unquestioning obedience. This is a necessary biological arrangement, as it provides safety for the group. Predators will naturally choose a single grey animal over a group.

Courting and Breeding

The true and good rooster presents a courting ritual to each female he wants to attract as one of his "wives." When the roos-

When a rooster finds a delicious bite to eat, he calls his hens with sounds resembling the clucking of a mother hen.

53

ter begins his courting dance, his posturing is characterized by a boldly upright stance, highly held head, visibly protruding chest, and a tip-toed dancelike stepping by which he moves around the desired female, always showing himself in profile—apparently he considers this the most impressive view of his efforts. He will perform this ritual as a morning greeting to each of his hens, and he will perform it again when a grateful hen accepts a favorite food morsel from his beak. During all of these activities, he makes a deep-throated pigeon-gurring sound, which we like to interpret as "Look how much I love you and how good I can be for you. . . !" It is interesting to observe how closely the behavior of the male now resembles that of a female towards her chicks: calling, offering of food morsels, huddling under the warmth of his wings. Just prior to the act of breeding (mating) the female, the male rushes toward her, often running into her in his excited haste. He then makes his courting sound again, gives the female a short push with his shoulder, and then mounts her from the back while she is crouching. The act of breeding lasts no more than a half minute altogether.

Depending on the individual and breed characteristics, there are also roosters that act so roughly that the hen cries out. Bantam males are not in the mood for breeding during the winter nor after molting. When the weather is cold and daylight time is short, the roosters forget about their gentleman's manners of wooing their hens, offering them tidbits, allowing them to eat first, and there is no mood for courting dances. However, males remain friendly toward their females.

Care of the Plumage

Healthy Banties clean and preen their feathers in a leisurely fashion several times every day. With their beaks they put each and every feather in its right place, and then they preen them by distributing oil over them, which serves as a protection against humidity and premature wear and tear. There is a gland at the base of the tail from which the bird extracts the necessary oily substance with its beak. On a Banty the gland is smaller than the size of a bean.

Caring for the plumage includes other behavioral characteristics, too—scratching the head, stretching and spreading the wings, stretching and picking legs and feet of the same side, and the vigorous shaking of the entire plumage.

Preening and cleaning activities are intensified during the molting season, when the old, loose feathers must be removed. In a typical good little chicken family, everyone helps each other with this important personal-care schedule. They do need each other because there are several spots on the head and neck that are very difficult to clean because neither beak nor toes can reach adequately. The receiving bird holds perfectly still, offering the neck and head side that needs to be groomed and, as you will observe, closes the eyes, showing contentment. In this way, hens take care of their roosters and also of each other, and the roosters re-

Padua Silver, female; the conceited upright carriage and the elongated rump are required by the various European Standards; this breed, however, is not recognized in the United States.

turn the favor in all gentility. When roosters are friendly with each other, especially when they have grown up with each other, they will also pick and preen each other's feathers. When you pet and gently scratch your Banties on heads and necks, they will similarly perceive this as a friendly favor.

During the molting season, the birds help each other with the removal of the cornified sheaths of the new feathers. While this is an essential procedure, it does not appear to be as pleasurable as the regular picking and preening rituals. You need to watch carefully to learn how to recognize when your Banties scratch and pick too often, because that would be an indication of parasitism which you would have to attend to immediately (see page 33).

Dust-Bathing

Dust-bathing is an integral part of personal chicken hygiene (see page 20). Bathing in water is not suitable. Dusting should be permitted only at temperatures above 68°F (20°C), preferably in warm, loose, and sandy earth. Dusting Banties scratch the ground where they like to dust, and they pick up sand and little stones at the same time. Then they whirl up the sand by fluffing and beating their wings, toes stretched backward, until the entire plumage is thoroughly

Behavioral Patterns of Bantams. Above left: This Padua hen is showing her chicks suitable foods; she picks up food pieces and lets them drop in front of the chicks. Above right: Cochins dusting. Below: Holland Gold-Necked, male and female scratching for food together; the male will tender an especially tasty morsel in his beak to the female.

"powdered." Subsequently they turn over on their side and back and huddle closely into the warm, sandy surface, visibly enjoying themselves with their eyes closed. Finally, they shake off all loose sand and dust.

Sensory Abilities

Sight: Banties are, like all birds, visually oriented—which is also true for humans. Chickens can distinguish the colors red, yellow, green, yellow-green, and blue-green, but not true blue. This fact makes it very useful to use blue light bulbs to warm a coop and for lighting at evening inspection visits.

The size of the eyeball permits visualization of a relatively large image. This accounts for the ability of chickens to see even the tiniest food particles, like seeds. They appear to recognize and differentiate among familiar persons by sight. This is thought to be true, also, for telling their own chicken mates from each other. It is typical that hens—who do not like each other—can be kept peaceful as long as they cannot see each other.

Hearing: Chickens do not hear as well as they can see, but their ears are reasonably well developed and useful. The mechanism of the ear contains a complex hearing system and also the specialized receptor cells for body-balancing and muscle-tensing. Chickens do not have the usual external ear. Instead, their external ear consists of an almost perfectly round opening that is surrounded by a disc and is hidden by tiny feathers all around.

Smelling (olfactory sense): The nasal cavity contains a mucous lining which holds

Understanding Bantams

the cells that make smelling possible. These are olfactory cells; the olfactory sense is poorly developed both in the nose and in the brain. Many experiments have documented the limited capacity of chickens to differentiate between scents.

Tasting: There is ample evidence for well-developed tasting abilities by the fact that chickens show definite tastes for favorite foods and decided refusal to drink foul-tasting water—even if the bird is thirsty. Chickens have taste buds like those of mammals; however, they are not found on the tongue but rather in the mucosal lining under the tongue, in the pharynx, and in the musculature of the pharynx.

Sound and Body Language

Chickens communicate by voice and gestures, and in this way they also show their moods. Other chickens as well as observant owners can understand these methods of communication.

• Crowing announces the morning just at the break of dawn. The type of crowing voice and the loudness vary. I recommend that you prepare your neighbors during a friendly conversation, and that you insulate the coop to diminish the external effect. Many Bantam breeds crow similarly to the wild breeds, whose crowing ends with a short, cut-off "Kee" phrase. Conversely, the large chicken breeds crow with an emphasis on long, extended end phase. The roosters of some breeds and varieties crow also during the day. This is usually not a frequent occurrence. It is used as an answering to calls of other males or as method of showing off to their harem-hens.

• The hen's loud, excited cackle announces an egg just laid. She goes on and on about it—sometimes for minutes on end. My hens quiet instantly as soon as I talk to them in a calming voice—and also when the rooster acknowledges them with a friendly "gogo-gohh" sound.

• Clucking sounds are the distinctive voice sounds of a broody hen and the contact assurance of a mother for her chicks. As soon as the chick starts chirping inside the egg, this clucking voice of the hen responds as a calming influence to assure that all is in order.

• There is also an accelerated sort of clucking mixed with excitement. That voice says "Come to eat!" It is fascinating to observe that this same manner of communication is also used by a caring rooster who wants to attract his hens. His voice is a little deeper, though—as his macho behavior demands. Even more interesting, both males and fe-

Healthy Banties clean themselves frequently—most preferably in the company of their "family."

58

Understanding Bantams

males use this familiar clucking sound to call "late" family members into the coop when it's time to sleep—amazingly, this sound always works!

• Whining-Clucking—a complaining clucking—that is as closely as I can describe it. Hens utter this typical clucking when they want to go back to their brood after an "outing." They also "say" this when an "empty brood nest" has been removed from under them. In the latter case they go back to normal after a day or two.

• There is an unharmonious screeching cackle made by hens who are "bothered" by males at the wrong time and in the wrong place, mainly when they are setting—and that sound is also heard when the intruder is a person looking or reaching into a brood nest.

• Hens will show affection and friendly, contented moods by vocalizing in a melodic singsong.

• The roosters call their hens with a long-drawn-out "gohhh."

• Both males and females utter an uncertain snarling deep-throated cackle when their coop seems strange or when it has been moved or when something unexpectedly appears suspicious—such as a change of food containers to a new shape, material, or color.

• The same snarling sonorous sound in a soft and gentle form is heard from my Bantam hens when I give them an unexpectedly delicious food morsel.

• Hens express their urgent wish for food, water, entry to the coop, or space in the nest box by calling in a monotonous nervy sound using one single tone.

• Utter fright and horror are expressed by both males and females alike by a high-pitched extended screaming cackle with a breaking pitch. This is what we experienced with our Banties when we first got them and they were frightened by dogs at the fence or cats that suddenly materialized in the yard. The entire reaction disappeared as the birds became more and more familiar with the four-legged critters that came by from time to time.

• Roosters express a particular type of anger and annoyance by a loud, throaty, screaming crow, during which they inhale at times and "trumpet" at others. This is not "fear," as the provoking sounds are not necessarily threatening or unfamiliar. The inducing factors may be just too much to endure, as, for example, the noise of airplanes breaking the sound barrier, construction noises, or similar "offenses." The rooster also complains in this manner when his hens do not arrive instantly upon his summons, when pigeons feed from his feeder, or when sparrows drink from his waterer.

• The situation where one of our Bantams is found speechless and entirely out of its depth leaves it with a silently open beak as some sort of desperate loss of communication.

• Head feathers standing on end coupled with a shivering all over the body indicates intense excitement and tension in both males and females.

• During normal times, all hens respect their ranking order. However, hens change their behavioral strategies while they are leading their chicks. At this time, it happens not infrequently that a lower-ranking female will attack or challenge a higher-ranking female or her human keeper—who in her eyes is also a higher-ranking "animal." This bold behavior is communicated by a conspicuously sideways ducked head, with the whole plumage seemingly standing on end, wings outstretched. A low-ranking mother with chicks will, at this time, scratch her keeper and try to get at the higher-ranking mother hen in whatever ways are open to her attacks.

Learning Abilities

Chickens are generally considered stupid; unfortunately, they are improperly compared with dogs and cats. With appropriate criteria in mind, however, it is a fact that chickens have very definite learning abilities.

Recognition
Chickens recognize each other as individuals. Observation has found that they can distinguish among up to 100 males. This process of recognition takes time. Males and females that you are planning to keep together should be brought together long before the season for laying and brooding. If a case of irreversible dislike arises, you will have to plan for separation and regrouping.

Chickens learn to be trusting and confiding with their owners/keepers if they are kept in a knowledgeable and gentle fashion. Visitors are quickly recognized as strangers.

Orientation
Chickens have a hard time adapting to new environmental conditions, such as a new coop in a different location. Breeders use this knowledge to prevent show birds

from laying eggs before they are shown. When I first had my Banties, I had to carry them into their coop every night—because they would not have wanted to go on their own into this new and strange house. This situation helped me at the same time to get them used to being carried by me. Pretty soon, they found their way home to the coop by themselves. By then, they knew every inch of the yard, the run, and the coop.

Awareness of Danger
At first our chickens were struck by panic any time a four-legged animal passed by. Slowly they learned that the fence kept them safe from dogs and they have learned to ignore both cats and dogs. It appears that such "enemy images" are genetically imprinted, and must be overcome by experience.

A crowing rooster expresses self-assurance and announces that he will defend hens, chicks, and territory from any rival.

Bantams from Around the World

Choosing the Best Strain

All Bantams are attractive to look at as the many color photos in this book will prove to you. There are too many breeds and varieties—up to 20 of one—to be described in a small volume such as this. On pages 64 and 65, I have compiled a list of various breeds with their characteristics and economic parameters—regardless of their color or beauty of appearance. The table lists important factors such as the number of eggs potentially produced per year; the average weights of males and females; feasibility as meat-chicken (quite rare!); broodiness; flight capacity; and characteristic traits.

For those readers who need to know the specific deficits for each breed in order to breed or produce, I advise the use of the *Standard*—a book published by the American Poultry Association.

There is a choice of breeds from either the group of the original Bantams or the group of bantamized large breeds. The seemingly unlimited number of varieties has evolved from the rich genetic material of the original wild chickens (see page 50).

Most breeds have several officially recognized color varieties and there are new varieties added constantly. Many breeds are tailored not only for their color, shape, and character, but also for their productivity: early maturation and egg yield. Sometimes it is hard to get all desirable characteristics bred into one bird, so that there will be breeds with magnificent coloration, yet with low egg production.

The index for the minimum weight of an egg suitable for incubation is not only impor-

tant for the resulting size of the chicks, but also gives an average value for egg sizes.

Setting hens do not lay eggs, which accounts for loss of productivity of about 10 to 12 weeks or of 2 to 4 weeks when an empty nest is removed. Most modern-day breeders prefer artificial incubation of eggs from hens that lack broodiness. This method allows more eggs to be incubated simultaneously and therefore an increased production of young chickens. This, in turn, provides larger numbers of show animals for exhibit from October through January. The first poultry show in the U.S. was held in Boston in 1849. The American Poultry Association was founded in Buffalo, New York, in 1873. At the poultry shows one can show off one's own creations and compare other breeders' work—and, above all, one may be rewarded with prizes and trophies for birds that are as exquisite as the Bantam *Standard* requires. The show is in fact an evaluation by comparison of the various Bantam breeds. Each chicken is housed in a separate wire coop, while individuals are grouped in classes according to age and sex within each variety. "A best-of-variety is then selected for com-

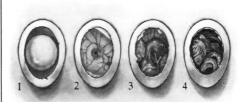

Development of a chick embryo during incubation:
1. First day (egg is not incubated) 2. Sixth day
3. Thirteenth day 4. Twentieth day (chick just before hatching)

Bantams from Around the World

petition with the other variety winners for best of breed, then continuing in the pyramid fashion up through breed groups until the overall champions are decided.''

Chickens fly better, higher, and more frequently during their first year than in later years. After the first year they rarely exceed the average flight capacity, except when they are scared, or when their run is too small and crowded. Some breeds remain confirmed and able flyers throughout their lives. For these you must provide aviary-style enclosures that are covered on all sides and on top.

There are descriptions of character on page 51 which declare a breed ''unaggressive'' or ''not shy''; these descriptions can only be relied upon when the keeping and husbandry are performed knowledgeably and gently. Gentleness is even required when you find Banties in your vegetable plot! Nervous behavior and excitement transfer quickly to chickens.

Killing and Butchering a Chicken

Chickens which are seriously ill, very old, very weak, or misformed can be humanely killed by a veterinarian. At this time, it would be kind of you to hold the tame and trusting animal in order to spare it the fear and excitement of a stranger's restraint.

Butchering is required for all overproduced birds and for most of the males, which hatch at a proportion of 1:1 with females. It is considered most humane to stun a chicken first by hitting it hard with a heavy object over the head, and only then cutting its throat and neck, and letting it bleed out.

Original Bantam Breeds

Ancona
U. S. *Standard* recognizes 1 variety. *Reproduction:* Good Layer; excellent brooding activities. Raises chicks well; easy to manage. Successful as foster mother; artificial incubation successful. *Flight capacity:* 4 to 5 feet (approximately 1.5 m) high; 6- to 8-foot fence recommended. *Character:* Alert and very active. Likes to fly! The male has large, white oval or almond-shaped earlobes and an evenly serrated and upright comb. *Special traits:* There are both single and rose-combed varieties. Matures quickly.

Bearded d'Anvers
(color photo, page 27) Recognized by U. S. *Standard. Reproduction:* Generally reliable but not for all color varieties; artificial incubation acceptable, but naturally bred birds are better. *Flight capacity:* About 6 feet (2 m) high; for city and suburban areas, aviary-style enclosure is advised. *Character:* Lively; tame; males sometimes aggressive.

Chabo
(color photo, page 27) U. S. *Standard* recognizes many colorful varieties. *Reproduction:* Reliable; artificial incubation successful. Homozygote offspring dies during embryonic stages or within one week after hatching. *Flight capacity:* 9 to 12 feet high (3–4 m); closed aviary-style housing required. Silkie and Curly varieties do not fly higher than 2 feet (60 cm). *Character:* Lively, tame, not aggressive. *Special traits:* Due to the particularly well-feathered legs and feet, it is essential to provide extremely dry and clean coop and run surfaces.

Bantams from Around the World

Cochin (Pekin)
(color photo, page 56 and inside back cover) U. S. *Standard* recognizes 5 varieties. *Reproduction:* Very reliable. Excellent brooding activities; also used for rearing other Bantam breeds or other game birds, such as pheasants; successful as foster mother; artificial incubation successful. *Flight capacity:* 2½ to 3 feet (80–100 cm) high. *Character:* Quiet, without being boring; males seldom aggressive. *Special traits:* The heavily feathered legs require extra-clean and dry floors in the coop and run.

Feather-Legged
(color photos, pages 9, 27, and front cover) Not recognized by U. S. *Standard.* *Reproduction:* There are not many breeding hens available, but when they do breed, their broods are successful; artificial incubation successful. *Flight capacity:* 6 feet (2 m) high. If there is ample space to run, the birds will respect a 6-foot fence limitation. *Character:* Lively and active; males try aggressive behavior but are relatively clumsy because of their heavily feathered feet.

Frizzle
U. S. *Standard* recognizes 3 varieties. *Reproduction:* Good brooding activities; successful as foster mother; artificial incubation successful. *Flight capacity:* 2 feet (60 cm) high. *Character:* Seldom aggressive. *Special traits:* A proper type has every feather curled (not ragged) in the direction opposite to normal; various colors. Whites are the best; black and blue are also popular.

German Bantam
(color photo, page 27) U. S. *Standard* recognizes 10 varieties. *Reproduction:* Natural and artificial incubation are both reliably successful. *Flight capacity:* Up to 24 feet (8 m) high. Covered enclosure mandatory. *Character:* Jaunty and active, with easily provoked aggressive males.

Holland
(color photo, page 56). U. S. *Standard* recognizes 10 varieties. *Reproduction:* Reliably successful. *Flight capacity:* Unlimited. Enclosures need to be covered in residential surroundings. *Character:* Very lively; males are aggressive even under calm conditions.

Java Bantam (Rosecomb)
U. S. *Standard* recognizes 8 varieties. *Reproduction:* Natural and artificial incubation both fairly successful. *Flight capacity:* 6 feet (2 m). *Character:* Lively; males are aggressive. *Special traits:* Long, tapering leader to the comb (leader: point at the rear of the comb which extends in a straight line). White earlobes, heavily furnished. Ornamental; doesn't need much space.

Ruhlaer
(color photo, page 27) German breed only. *Reproduction:* Consistently successful. Chicks that are homozygous for tail-loss will die during embryonic development or shortly after hatching. *Flight capacity:* 9 feet (3 m) high. Covered enclosure required in residential areas. *Character:* Very lively; some males are aggressive. *Special trait:* Strong egg-layers during winter months.

Sebright
U. S. *Standard* recognizes 3 varieties. *Reproduction:* Often infertile eggs; moderate rearability; artificial incubation frequently necessary. *Flight capacity:* 6 to 15 feet (2–5 m). Aviary-style enclosure advised. *Character:* Very lively; some males are aggressive. *Special traits:* Ornamental; rose

Bantam Varieties: Facts and Figures

	Colors	Average body weight: oz.		Maturation time (months)		First eggs laid (months)	Minimum egg weight for breeding: -oz. (g)	Eggshell color and number of eggs per year
Original Bantam Breeds		♂	♀	♂	♀			
Ancona	2	32	25	5	5	5	1.0 (30)	White/180–200
Bearded d'Anvers	10	23	19	5–6	5–6	5–6	.9 (25)	White-cream/80–120
Chabo	13	21	18	6	5	5	1.0 (28)	Yellow-cream-white/80–100
Cochin (Pekin)	15	30	26	10	6–7	6–8	1.0 (30)	Beige-brown/100–200
Feather-legged	14	25	21	6	6	6	1.0 (30)	Whitish/120
German	13	25	21	7–8	5–6	7–10	1.0 (30)	White-cream-light brown/60–150
Holland	10	26	19	6	6	6	1.0 (30)	Whitish/120
Ruhlaer	19	32	25	9	9	9–10	1.4 (40)	White/150
Sebright	2	21	18	6	5	5–6	1.0 (30)	White-cream/60–80
Silkies	5	35	28	5½	5	5–5½	1.2 (35)	Brownish/90–120

	Colors	Average body weight: oz.		Maturation time (months)		First eggs laid (months)	Minimum egg weight for breeding: -oz. (g)	Eggshell color and number of eggs per year
Bantamized Large Breeds								
Amrocks	1	35	32	5	4½	5	1.4 (40)	Brownish/yellowish, 200 and more
Andalusian	1	32	28	5	4	5	1.5 (42)	White/120
Araucana	3	28	21	9	8	6	1.0 (30)	Turquoise/150–180
Barnevelder	3	35	32	5	5	5	1.4 (40)	Brown/120 and over 200
Brabanter	9	35	28	8–9	8–9	9	1.4 (40)	White/150
Brahma	3	38	35	8	7	7–8	1.2 (35)	Light brown/190
Salmon Faverolle	2	35	32	5	4½	4½	1.3 (38)	Light yellow-brown/160–190
Indian Game	3	39	32	5	5	5	1.2 (35)	Yellow-brown, brown/60–80
Modern English Game	14	21	18	5	4	5	.9 (25)	White-yellowish brown/50–70
Old English Game	20	28	25	5	4	4	1.0 (30)	White-yellowish brown/60–80
Hamburgh	3	35	28	6	6	6	1.4 (40)	White/130

Bantam Varieties: Facts and Figures

	Colors	Average body weight: oz.		Maturation time (months)		First eggs laid (months)	Minimum egg weight (for breeding: -oz.(g))	Eggshell color and number of eggs per year
		♂	♀	♂	♀			
Holland White-Crested	5	32	28	7	6	6	1.4 (40)	White/100–140
Italian	15	35	32	6	5	5–6	1.2 (35)	White/140
Kraaikop	2	30	26	7	6	5–6	1.2 (35)	Yellowish/120–140
La Fleche	1	49	42	10	10	10	1.5 (42)	White/200
Lakenfelder	1	28	25	6	6	6½	1.0 (30)	White–yellow/160
Langschan	7	35	25	8	7	6	1.2 (35)	Brownish/160
Leghorn	1	28	25	6–7	5–6	5–6	1.2 (35)	White/130/180
Minorca	2	32	28	5–6	5	5	1.2 (35)	White/more than 150
East Friesian Moeven	2	28	25	6	5–5½	5	1.2 (35)	White/120–140
Naked Neck	7	28	25	5	4	6	1.0 (30)	White/100–120
New Hampshire	2	39	28	5	4–5	4–5	1.4 (40)	Brown/180
Orloff	3	35	28	7	6	6	1.2 (35)	Whitish/brownish/120–150
Orpington	7	35	32	8	6	4–5	1.2 (35)	Light beige/160–180
Padua	7	32	28	7	6	6	1.2 (35)	White/90–110
Phoenix	5	28	25	8	6	6–7	.9 (25)	White/80–100
Plymouth Rock	5	35	28	7	6	5½	1.4 (40)	Yellowish/160
German Reichshuhn	7	35	28	6½	5½	5½	1.4 (40)	Yellowish/140-150
Rhode Island	1	35	28	6½	5½	6	1.4 (40)	Light brown/180
German Sperber	1	32	28	6	5	4½	1.4 (40)	White/180
Sussex	4	46	35	6	5	5–6	1.4 (40)	Light yellow-brown/150–180
Bearded Thuringer	8	28	25	6		6	1.0 (30)	White/140–160
Welsumer	2	35	32	5	4½		1.6 (45)	Reddish-brown/180
Wyandotte	18	35	28	6	5		1.4 (40)	Brownish/100–180
Yokohama	2	28	25	12	5–6		1.0 (30)	Yellowish/40–120

combs. Males lack the pointed, long hackle feathers and flowing tails.

Silkie

(color photo, page 45) U. S. *Standard* recognizes 10 varieties. *Reproduction:* Very consistent. Highly successful as foster mothers for other Banties or other birds. Artificial incubation successful. *Flight capacity:* 3 feet (1 m) at most. *Character:* Quiet, very tame.

Sumatra

U. S. *Standard* recognizes 1 variety. *Reproduction:* Excellent layer; natural and artificial incubation are reliably successful. *Flight capacity:* 6 feet (2 m). *Character:* Lively and active. *Special traits:* Completely black; small pealike combs; strong legs. Cocks should carry their tails horizontally or in line with the back.

Bantamized Large Breeds

Amrocks

(color photo, page 10 and back cover) Not recognized by U. S. *Standard*. *Reproduction:* Minimal brooding activities; require artificial incubation. *Flight capacity:* About 3 feet (1 m) high. A fence of 4.5 feet is sufficient limitation. *Character:* Quiet, calm, and tame when treated gently.

Andalusian

Recognized by U. S. *Standard*. *Reproduction:* Despite missing brooding desire, they raise chicks well after artificial incubation. The Andalusian Blue—which is a dove-blue version with distinct black framing of each feather—divides into 50% blue, 25% black, 25% white, which leads to 50% ''pure'' chicks. *Flight capacity:* 4 to 5 feet (1.5 m) high; 6-foot fence recommended.

Character: Very jaunty and active; roosters get quite cheeky at times!

Araucana

(color photo, page 45) U. S. *Standard* recognizes 1 variety. *Reproduction:* Not all hens will set. Artificial incubation customary. Lethal genes go with tailless and curly-feathered offspring. *Flight capacity:* Unlimited; covered enclosures are important in residential areas, preferably with tree growth inside the run. *Character:* Calm and tame with gentle caretakers; aggressive at sudden or frightening events.

Barnevelder

U.S. *Standard* recognizes 2 varieties. *Reproduction:* Poor breeding activity, but successful hatching ratio and good parenting. Artificial incubation is customary. *Flight capacity:* Just above 3 feet (1 m); a fence of 4 to 5 feet is sufficient. *Character:* Quiet, tame without aggressive tendencies.

Brabanter

(color photo, page 46) This is a Belgian Bantam—not recognized by U. S. *Standard*. *Reproduction:* Minimal and inconsistent brooding behavior requires artificial incubation and raising of the chicks. *Flight capacity:* 9 feet (3 m) high; requires covered runs in residential areas. *Character:* Lively; tame with gentle keepers. Males are naturally aggressive. *Special traits:* The crest is easily infested with parasites and requires frequent inspection, combing, and general cleanliness.

Brahma

(color photo, page 10) U. S. *Standard* recognizes 5 varieties. *Reproduction:* Very consistent; artificial incubation not necessary.

Bantams from Around the World

Flight capacity: Minimal: A fence of 3 to 4 feet (1.20 m) suffices. *Character:* Quiet, tame males when treated gently. *Special traits:* Good for meat production; the heavily feathered legs require extra clean and dry floors in the coop and run.

Dorking

U. S. *Standard* recognizes 1 variety. *Reproduction:* Normal and artificial methods successful. *Flight capacity:* 3 feet (1 m), requiring 3 to 4-foot fence at most. *Character:* Males are friendly and not at all aggressive. *Special traits:* Five toes on each foot; the fifth one rising from the back toe. Heavy breed; long and deep body. Only one color: the silver gray (modified duckwing).

Faverolle

U. S. *Standard* recognizes 3 varieties. *Reproduction:* Excellent brooding activities; fairly large eggs; successful as foster mother; artificial incubation successful. *Flight capacity:* 2 feet (60 cm) high. *Character:* Active, hardy, and fertile. Extra toe; leg feathers; fully muffled face.

Salmon Faverolle

(color photo, page 10) Not recognized by U. S. *Standard. Reproduction:* Inconsistent; requires artificial incubation. *Flight capacity:* Approximately 3 feet (1 m) high, requiring a fence of not more than 4 to 5 feet (1.5 m). *Character:* Under gentle handling, quiet, confiding nature. *Special traits:* Good for meat production; young males are early recognizable by characteristically dark feathers on wings and shoulders.

Indian Game

U. S. *Standard* recognizes 2 varieties. *Reproduction:* Not remarkable layer, although some suitable hens are available.

Flight capacity: 3 feet (1 m) high, requiring a 3-foot fence at most. *Character:* Not aggressive. *Special traits:* Heavy, blocky (thick-set) breed. Pealike combs, heavy heads, and light-colored eyes; close and waxy plumage. Originated in England.

Modern English Game

(color photo, page 45) *Reproduction:* Natural and artificial methods are both successful. *Flight capacity:* 6 to 9 feet (2– 3 m) high, requiring aviary-type enclosure in suburban setting. *Special traits:* These birds require a minimum of 54°F to 59°F (12°–15°C) temperature and must be treated thermostatically when necessary.

Old English Game

U. S. *Standard* recognizes 29 varieties. *Reproduction:* Consistent, successful natural reproduction; artificial incubation feasible, but less successful. *Flight capacity:* Up to 9 feet (3 m) high; require aviary. *Character:* Under gentle caretaking habits these birds are quiet and friendly. Their aggressive behavior is playful and enjoyably bold.

Hamburgh

U. S. *Standard* recognizes 6 varieties. *Reproduction:* Poor natural reproductive behavior requires artificial incubation. *Flight capacity:* 9 feet (3 m) high; requires aviary-style enclosure. *Character:* Lively and tame; when treated gently they are not aggressive.

Holland White-Crested

(color photos pages 9, 27, 28, and back cover) *Reproduction:* Artificial incubation and rearing necessary. Chicks are excessively susceptible to colds. New crests must be trimmed. A dry and well-protected run is essential. *Flight capacity:* 3 feet (1 m) high, requiring a fence of about 4 feet (1.2 m).

Bantams from Around the World

Special traits: Crests need frequent inspection for parasites and require immediate treatment when affected.

Italian

(color photo, page 10) Not recognized by U. S. *Standard. Reproduction:* Artificial incubation and rearing required. *Flight capacity:* 6 to 9 feet (2–3 m) high; requires aviary-style enclosure in residential areas. *Character:* Lively, easily frightened; tends to shy behavior when the keeper uses rough handling methods.

Kraaikop

(color photo, page 46) Dutch origin. U. S. *Standard* recognizes 2 varieties. *Reproduction:* Mostly successful natural and artificial incubation. *Flight capacity:* 9 feet (3 m) high, requiring cover enclosure in suburban areas. *Character:* Genetic fighting-game qualities give these birds a truly lively character, yet tame when treated gently. Individual males show some aggression.

La Fleche

(color photo, page 45) U. S. *Standard* recognizes 1 variety (black). *Reproduction:* Brooding hens are not available, and artificial incubation is necessary. *Flight capacity:* 9 feet (3 m) high, requiring aviary in residential areas. *Character:* Males are not aggressive. *Special traits:* V-shaped, hornlike combs; the small crests must be inspected frequently for parasites; high egg production during winter.

Lakenfelder

U. S. *Standard* recognizes 1 variety. *Reproduction:* Lack of brooding hens requires artificial incubation. *Flight capacity:* Unlimited; requires aviary conditions. *Character:* Quiet, calm; shyer than others.

Langschan

U. S. *Standard* recognizes 3 varieties. *Reproduction:* Natural reproduction pattern highly successful. *Flight capacity:* Low heights; a fence of 3 feet is sufficient. *Character:* Quiet, friendly, unaggressive.

Leghorn

(color photo, page 46) U. S. *Standard* recognizes 23 varieties. *Reproduction:* Lack of brooding hens makes artificial incubation essential. *Flight capacity:* 4 to 5 feet (1.5 m) high; fencing of 6 feet is adequate. *Character:* Lively but easily frightened; males are more shy than aggressive.

Malays

U. S. *Standard* recognizes 2 varieties. *Reproduction:* Natural and artificial incubation successful. *Flight capacity:* 3 to 6 feet (1–2 m) high; require fencing of about 7 feet. *Character:* Aggressive. *Special traits:* Fierce expression; pale eyes. Sparsely feathered; walnut combs. Tall and heavily boned. Various colors: black-red, cinnamon, white, and spangled. The last two are very popular in England.

Marans

U. S. *Standard* recognizes 3 varieties. *Reproduction:* Excellent layers; often used for rearing pheasants and other game birds. *Flight capacity:* 3 feet (1 m) high, requiring a 3-foot fence at most. *Character:* Hardy, docile, easy to manage. *Special traits:* Heavy breed; white skin and legs; single comb. Various colors: the dark cuckoo, golden, and silver cuckoo are the most famous.

Minorca

U. S. *Standard* recognizes 6 varieties. *Reproduction:* Natural reproductive results

Bantams from Around the World

are poor; artificial incubation recommended. *Flight capacity:* Unlimited; aviary required as enclosure. *Character:* Lively, but males are not aggressive when handled gently.

East Friesian Moeven

(color photo, page 10) U. S. *Standard* recognizes 3 varieties. *Reproduction:* Natural, reliably successful; artificial methods feasible. *Flight capacity:* 9 feet (3 m) high, requiring an aviary. *Character:* Jaunty but peaceful and confiding, males as well as females. *Special traits:* Golden-necked varieties are a little weaker than silver-necks.

Naked Neck

U. S. *Standard* recognizes 6 varieties. *Reproduction:* Hens for natural reproduction not available; artificial reproduction necessary. *Flight capacity:* Unlimited; aviary needed for suburban areas. *Character:* Lively but unaggressive males.

New Hampshire

(color photo, page 10) U. S. *Standard* recognizes 1 variety. *Reproduction:* Natural production is unreliable; artificial reproduction is more customary. *Flight capacity:* Not more than 6 feet (2 m) high; fence should be about 7 feet. *Character:* Lively, tame, and trusting; males get along with each other after some time of familiarization. The males are not aggressive toward people.

Orloff

U. S. *Standard* recognizes 3 varieties. *Reproduction:* Some suitable hens are available but artificial incubation and raising is more frequent. *Flight capacity:* Moderate heights; a fence of about 4 to 5 feet (1.5 m) is adequate. *Character:* Lively; distinctly jaunty game-bird behavior; rarely aggressive toward keepers.

Orpington

(color photo, page 45) U. S. *Standard* recognizes 4 varieties. *Reproduction:* Both natural and artificial methods are successful. *Flight capacity:* Below 3 feet (1 m), requiring a 3-foot fence at most. *Character:* Calm; not aggressive, yet lively. *Special traits:* High egg production in winter; suitable as meat.

Padua

(color photos, pages 55, 56) Not recognized by U. S. *Standard*. *Reproduction:* Artificial method only. Offspring with homozygote nasal enlargement is lethal. *Flight capacity:* 6 feet (2 m) high; fence should be a little higher than 6 feet. *Character:* With proper care, all birds are friendly, unaggressive. *Special traits:* Frequent inspection of the crest to check for parasites. Regular combing and treatment as soon as it may be needed.

Phoenix

(color photo, page 46) U. S. *Standard* recognizes 6 varieties. *Reproduction:* Natural reproduction restricts need for artificial incubation to winter broods. *Flight capacity:* More than 9 feet (3 m) high; aviary required. *Character:* Lively but easily frightened; gentle and confiding under good care. Though there is a distinct fighting-game quality, the roosters are rarely aggressive. *Special trait:* Coop and run must be extraordinarily clean and dry to keep these Bantams' beautiful, long tails undamaged.

Plymouth Rock

U. S. *Standard* recognizes 7 varieties. *Reproduction:* Rarely natural, although successful when hen is broody; artificial incubation more customary. *Flight capacity:* Low

Bantams from Around the World

flying, if at all—a fence of 3 to 4 feet is more than enough. *Character:* Lively and friendly, and very confiding with gentle keepers.

Poland

U. S. *Standard* recognizes 4 varieties. *Reproduction:* Excellent layer. *Flight capacity:* 6 to 15 feet (2–5 m) high. Aviary-style enclosure advised. *Character:* Lively; tame; males sometimes aggressive. *Special traits:* Ornamental; considered to be the most highly developed of all breeds with crests. Various colors: white-crested blacks and blues (with plain faces), self-colors and laced (both muffled and crested.)

German Reichshuhn

(Color photo, page 45) *Reproduction:* Natural and artificial methods are both successful. *Flight capacity:* 4 feet (1.20 m) high; a fence of 5 feet (1.6 m) is sufficient. *Character:* Males are trusting with gentle keepers but shy otherwise; never aggressive.

Rhode Island

U. S. *Standard* recognizes 2 Reds, 2 Whites. *Reproduction:* Natural and artificial materials are both successful. *Flight capacity:* Rarely more than 3 feet (1 m) high; a fence of 4 feet is sufficient. *Character:* Friendly, quiet, trusting; males not aggressive.

German Sperber

Not recognized by U. S. *Standard.* *Reproduction:* Mainly artificial; nice hens are rarely available. *Flight capacity:* 9 to 12 feet (3–4 m) high, needs aviary-type enclosure. *Character:* Lively, quickly tame and trusting; males are not aggressive.

Sussex

(color photo, page 46) U. S. *Standard* recognizes 7 varieties. *Reproduction:* Natural reproduction very successful, artificial incubation feasible but not necessary. *Flight capacity:* Under 5 feet (1.5 m), requiring a fence of more than 5 feet. *Character:* Males are not aggressive.

Bearded Thuringer

U. S. *Standard* recognizes 5 varieties. *Reproduction:* Few hens available but successful when found; artificial incubation more frequent. *Flight capacity:* Unlimited, requiring covered enclosures. *Character:* Trusting and lively, not aggressive.

Welsumer

Recognized by U. S. *Standard. Reproduction:* Very few hens available, but they are successful; artificial incubation feasible and customary. *Flight capacity:* More than 5 feet (1.7 m) high; requiring a fence of about 6 feet. *Character:* Despite their jaunty behavior they are not aggressive.

Wyandotte

(color photo, page 46) U. S. *Standard* recognizes 18 varieties. *Reproduction:* Normal and artificial methods both consistently successful. *Flight capacity:* Relatively low; a fence of 3 to 4 feet is sufficient. *Character:* Males are friendly and not at all aggressive.

Yokohama

(color photo, page 28) Not recognized by U. S. *Standard. Reproduction:* Very consistent and reliable natural breeding behavior. *Flight capacity:* Not more than 3 feet (1 m) high. *Character:* Fighting game-bird characteristics, with male aggressive inclination. As fighting game, they are typically muscular and wiry with straight, hard feathers. Aggressive toward their own kind.

Index

Numerals in *italics* indicate color photographs
Accessories, 18–20
Accident prevention, 22
Adults, food for, 26
American Poultry Association, 61
Amrock, *10*, 66
Ancestral Bantam, *27*
Ancestral chickens, 50
Ancona, 62
Andalusian, 66
Animal protein, 23, 25
Araucana, 66
Artificial incubation, 39
Attack position, *9*
Automatic waterers, 19

Bankiva, 50
Bantamized large breeds, 66–70
Barnevelder, 66
Bearded d'Anvers (*Barbus d'Anvers*), *27*, 62
Bearded Thuringer, 70
Behavior:
    during courting, 53
    of chicks, 44, 47–49
    of hens, 52–53
    of roosters, 53
Blastoderm, 40–41
Body language, 59–60
Brabanter, 46, 66
Brahma, *10*, 66–67
Breed chart, 64–65
Breeding:
artificial incubation, 39
broodiness, 38
    chick embryo development, 41
    chicks, hatching and growth of, 43–44, 47–49
    considerations before, 36
    fertile eggs, 39–41
    fertilization, 37–38
    husbandry chores for setting, 41–42
    pairing and brooding, 37
    prerequisites for, 36–37
    production capacity, 37
    setting, 38–39
    setting hen, 42–43
    storing eggs, 40
Brooder box, 17

Brooders, 20
Broodiness, 38
Brooding instinct, 37
Brown eggs, 40
Butchering a chicken, 62

Cackle, 58
Candling, 41
Care, 11–22
Carrying baskets, 20
Carrying method, 22
Cats, 6
Cecal worm, 33
Chabo, *27*, 52, 62
Chick embryo, 41
Chicken family, 51
Chicken feeders, 18
Chick pen, 17
Chicks:
    behavior of, 44, 47–49
    food and nutrition for, 24–25
    hatching of, 43–44
Clucking, 58
Coccidiosis, 31
Cochin, 51, *56*, 63
Communication, 58–60
Coop:
    correct size, 11
    flooring and roofing, 12–13
    foundations, 12
    heating and lighting of, 14
    litter, 15
    location of, 11
    perches, 15
    surface treatment and insulation, 12
    ventilation, 14
    walls, 11
    windows and doors, 13–14
Courting behavior, 53–54
Crested Bantam, *27*
Crowing, 58
Crowing Feather-Legged Bantam, *9*

Danger, awareness of, 60
Death, by freezing, 29
Digestion, 23
Diseases:
    chart of, 32
    coccidiosis, 31
    infectious hepatitis, 31
    parasites, 33–35

Marek's disease, 31
Disinfection, 35
Dogs, 5–6
Domestication, 50–51
Dorking, 67
Drinking water requirements, 26
Dropping pits, 15
Dust bath, 20
Dust bathing, 57
Dust pen, 20

East Friesian Moeven, *10*, 69
Egg production capacity, 37
Egg storage, 40
Egg traps, 20
External parasites (ectoparasites), 34–35

Faverolle, 67
Feather-legged, *9*, *27*, 63
Feather mites, 34
Fecal testing, 29
Feed bowls, 18–19
Feeder boards, 18
Feeding rules, 23–24
Fenced run, 16–17
Fertile eggs, 39–40
Fertilization, 37–38
Fighting for ranking order, 51–52
First-aid, 30–31
First egg, 37
Fleas, 34
Flies, 35
Floating embryonated eggs, 42
Food intake, 26
Foods *See* Nutrition
Forktail, 50
Free-ranging run, 16
Frizzle, 63
Frostbite, 29

German Bantam, *27*, *45*, 63
German Sperber, 70
Gizzard, 23
Greens, 23–26
Grit, 23
Guinea pigs, 6

Hamburgh, 67
Hanging baskets, 18–19
Healthy chicken, recognition of, 7

Hearing, 57
Heating and lighting, 14
Hen behavior, 52–53
Hen house, 17–18
Holland, *27*, 63
Holland Gold-Necked, *56*
Holland White-Crested, *9*, *27*, *28*, 67–68
Home transport, 8
Hookworms, 33
Husbandry, 11–22
Hygiene, 15

Illness *See* Diseases; Sickness
Incubators, 20
Indian Game, 67
Infectious catarrh (rup), 33
Infectious hepatitis, 31
Infrared lamp, 20
Initial care, 8
Internal parasites (endoparasites), 33–34
Italian, *10*, 68

Java Bantam (Rosecomb), 63

Killing a chicken, 62
Kraaikop, 46, 68

Lafayette, 50
La Fleche, *45*, 68
Lakenfelder, 68
Langschan, 68
Learning abilities, 60
Leg bands, 49
Leghorn, *46*, 68
Light cycle, 14
Lighting, 14
Litter, 15

Malays, 68
Marans, 68
Marek's disease, 31
Minerals, 23
Minorca, 68–69
Modern English Game, *45*, 67
Molting (annual), 30
Molting season, 57

Nail clippers, 20
Naked Neck, 69
Nesting boxes, 19–20
Nests, 19–20
New Hampshire, *10*, 69

Index

Nutrition:
  for adults, 26
  for chicks, 24–25
  digestion, 23
  drinking water
    requirements, 26
  feeding rules, 23–24
  food supplements, 26
  right food, 23
  for young bantams, 25

Old English Game, 67
Olfactory cells, 58
Orientation, 59
Orloff, 69
Orpington, 45, 69

Padua, 55, 56, 69
Padua Silver, 55
Pairing instinct, 37
Parasites, 33–35
Perches, 15
Pets and Bantams, 5–6
Pheasant food, 24
Phoenix, 46, 69
Plumage, care of, 54, 57
Plymouth Rock, 69–70
Poland, 70
Poultry breeders associations,
  36
Preening gland, 54
Preventriculus, 23
Purchase, 7

Rabbits, 6
Ranking order, 51–52
Recognition, 59
Red bird mites, 34
Reproduction See Breeding
Rhode Island, 70
Rooster behavior, 53–54
Roundworms, 33
Ruhlaer, 27, 63
Runs, 16–17

Salmon Faverolle, 10, 67
Sanitation, 35
Scaly leg mites, 34
Scratch, 23–26
Sebright, 63, 66
Sensory abilities, 57–58
Setting, 38–39

Setting hen:
  care of, 42
  nest box for, 42
  work of, 42–43
Shows, 36–37, 61–62
Sickness, prevention of, 29
  See also Diseases
Sight, 57
Silkie, 45, 51, 66
Smell, sense of, 57–58
Social animal, 51
Sonnerath, 50
Sounds, 58–59
Special requirements, runs
  for, 17
Standard of Perfection,
  36, 61
Strain, choosing the best,
  61–62
Sumatra, 66
Supplements, 25, 26
Sussex, 46, 70

Tapeworms, 33–34
Taste, sense of, 58
Temperature requirements,
  21–22
Thermometer, 20
Thermostatic-controlled
  heater, 14, 20
Ticks, 35
Tracheal worms, 33
Turtles, 6

Unfertile eggs, 41

Vacation, planning for, 6
Ventilation, 14

Waterers, 19
Welsumer, 70
Whining-clucking sound, 59
Wyandotte, 46, 70

Yokohama, 28, 70

Publications

Bantam Standard
American Bantam Association, Box 464,
Chicago, Illinois 60690. Carries an orga-
nized sequence of lessons on conditioning,
breeding, mating, growing, etc. The Association also issues a yearbook.

The Poultry Fancier
B.K.T. Publishing Co., Eanam, Blackburn,
Lancs. England. Monthly.

Poultry Press
Box 947, York, Pennsylvania 17405.
The newspaper contains announcements of
poultry shows throughout the country, man-
agement informations, general news, tips on
care, classified advertising. Monthly.

Equipment and Supplies

Brower Manufacturing Company
640 South Fifth Street,
Quincy, Illinois 62301.
Poultry equipment (incubators, feeders,
waterers, water heating devices, etc.)

March Manufacturing Inc.,
14232 Brookhurst Street,
Garden Grove, California 92643.
Books, incubators, brooders, nets, etc.

Rocky Top Poultry Supplies
PO Box 1006,
Harriman,
Tennessee 37748.
Books, cages, automatic watering devices,
incubators, etc.